The Call

The Call

Theresa Tulloch

Copyright © 2022 by Theresa Tulloch.

Library of Congress Control Number:		2022921033
ISBN:	Hardcover	978-1-6698-5495-1
	Softcover	978-1-6698-5494-4
	eBook	978-1-6698-5493-7

All rights reserved. No part of this book may be reproduced or transmitted in any form or by any means, electronic or mechanical, including photocopying, recording, or by any information storage and retrieval system, without permission in writing from the copyright owner.

Holy Bible, New International Version®, NIV® Copyright ©1973, 1978, 1984, 2011 by Biblica, Inc.® Used by permission. All rights reserved worldwide.

Any people depicted in stock imagery provided by Getty Images are models, and such images are being used for illustrative purposes only.
Certain stock imagery © Getty Images.

Cover Photo by Justin Gladden

Print information available on the last page.

Rev. date: 11/09/2022

To order additional copies of this book, contact:
Xlibris
844-714-8691
www.Xlibris.com
Orders@Xlibris.com
844729

CONTENTS

About the Book vii

Chapter 1 Migration 1
Chapter 2 The Foundation 6
Chapter 3 From the Outside 28
Chapter 4 Success: Whose Standards 36
Chapter 5 Working for My Good 43
Chapter 6 Really, Really 52
Chapter 7 No Means No! 72
Chapter 8 2020: From Darkness to Light 75
Chapter 9 Just Being 90

Acknowledgments 113

ABOUT THE BOOK

THIS BOOK IS about a woman's journey of faith that stemmed from coping with the effects of childhood trauma and trials to being triumphant over obstacles that ultimately led to her divine purpose.

To my two beautiful children Tracy and Terrence. I love you both very much. I pray that as you go on your own journey of faith, you remember to use the tools that were given to me for strength and encouragement.

CHAPTER 1

Migration

ALTHOUGH MY FAMILY migrated from Jamaica to the United States when I was six years old, I have some vivid memories of my early childhood there. I recall living in a house surrounded by tangerine or orange trees in the backyard that resembled a forest, and we had a huge backyard that we played in most of the day. I was born in the house that we lived in at 9 Charlton Road Kingston 8, Jamaica, which is really in St. Andrews, Jamaica. It was a large house with three sections: the main house with an upstairs where the landlord lived, the upper level rented to another older lady, and then there was an additional wing where we lived. At first, it was Ma, Dad, Ingrid, Denise, and me.

We were poor, but I did not realize it because we were happy. I remember Dad left the year before we migrated to America. It was the custom of families migrating to America or England to send one parent or spouse ahead, so he or she could establish himself. Then the following year, the children and spouses would migrate. I don't remember the events leading up to his leaving, but I recall Denise always complaining to Ma about why she sent her daddy away. Denise, my sister who is a year older than me, was very feisty. She would fuss at Ma, and every day say in Patois (Jamaican dialect), "Weh mi daddi de, mi wan mi daddy! You mek dem tek weh mi daddy." I remember Ma feeling very bad and trying to pacify Denise by bringing her to work with her. And my mother's coworkers would give my sister money.

We had a large yard, which was situated at the front and side of the house. We climbed the cherry trees, picked cherries, and set up a table in front of our house to sell. Friends from down the block and a few houses down spent every day with us because we had a big yard. We dominated that yard because the landlord was an old lady who didn't come out of the house and had no use for the space.

We had an only-child friend who lived with her grandmother up the block. We thought she was rich because her foreign mother (American) would send real dolls to her, not like the cloth and mop-string-haired ones my mom made us. She had china dishware and toys from America to play with. Her grandmother had no use for the household items, so our friend would bring real plates, cups, and eating utensils over for us to play with. These items also came in handy when we set up shop in front of our gate to sell cherries. Life was so exciting, and we acted grown up, but we were innocent.

One of my fondest memories growing up in Jamaica was the Christmas Day of December 1980. Ma worked at Kentucky Fried Chicken for the evening shift, from 4:00 p.m. to 11:00 p.m., so she always got to bring home leftover food that didn't sell. Our cousin, Steve, who was just about seventeen years old, lived with us when Dad migrated to America. He was so helpful to Ma and us. Besides free Kentucky Fried Chicken, we did not have a lot of food, but we would provoke him to make fried dumplings. He would take the little bit of flour we had and make huge dumplings for us to share. He took good care of us since Ma had four children and Dad was away in America.

The night before Christmas, Ma came home with buckets of chicken from work. That was our Christmas gift. We had so much chicken that on Christmas Day, we set up a table in front of our gate and served, not sold, chicken to people who passed by. We had decorations from our friend up the block and celebrated Christmas with our friends and neighbors right in front of the house. The neighbors admired us because we were children doing our thing. They also knew we were going to foreign ("foreign" is the Jamaican vernacular used for families abroad in America or England), and they were happy for us. It is a big deal whenever a family is granted a visa or what is known as a green card to migrate to another country. Often, the remaining family, friends, and neighbors would celebrate and ask the migrating family to remember them. This is why, oftentimes, Caribbean families in American spend a lot of money shipping barrels back to their home country for family and friends left behind.

Another fond memory I have was when Ma came home from the hospital after having Kimone. This was in January 1980. She had a caesarean, and her stomach was bandaged up. Denise and I had to stay in Portland (country) while she recovered. We were sent to the country to stay with our great-grandparents while Ma recuperated from her cesarean with Kimone. Ingrid was nine years old at the time and stayed behind with Ma to help take care of her. Dad was already in America, preparing the way for us to come. After the caesarean, Ma couldn't manage all four of us by herself.

The country was amazing. Mommi and Pappi (my great-grandparents on Ma's side) allowed us to play freely outside. The house was on a hill that overlooked the roads, valley, and everything else. There was a small creek just below the house. This is where they would fish for shrimp to cook. There was a pit toilet (outdoor bathroom) and an outside pipe for washing. My great-grandparents were poor but we did not know it because we had plenty of fruit to eat. The house was in the middle of a forest on a hill surrounded by oranges, grapefruits, tangerines, naseberries, and genip trees. We played outside and ran up and down the hill most of the day unless it rained.

My great-grandparents were very old but energetic and loving. I recall the smell of Mommi's fried dumplings, cooked *boosu* (like shrimp), and the smell of her cooking with coconut oil. It is amazing how great of a cook my great-grandmother was. She cooked everything outside. She cut and grated the coconut herself. She took pride in grating the cocoa to make cocoa tea. They did not have an inside kitchen or electric appliances, much less a gas stove, yet the rice and food came out perfect. We were so busy playing in the dirt with sticks and anything we found outside—picking fruit, and enjoying the country life—that we did not miss having toys or other things children had to entertain themselves with. We were happy.

I recall Poppi always stopping what he was doing to pray at the same time every day, which I later found out was his 6:00 p.m. prayer time. I recall him saying in his daily prayer, "Bless mi pickney, pickney, and bless mi pickney, pickney, pickney, pickney!" He would get on his knees, and he was so loud that his tenor voice frightened me. I didn't realize, until years later, that Poppi was praying for his grandchildren's children and the unborn generation to come.

From my observation of my great-grandfather's prayer, a seed of growing to pray was planted. It is not a coincidence that on the 6:00 a.m. hour, I also pray so loudly that my mother, whose bedroom is underneath the room where I pray, says I wake her up, but she does not mind! In this life, there are no coincidences. God unfolds our journey through trials, tests, and experiences outside of our actions. Eventually, these experiences make a great connection that leads to our purposes.

My greatest memory of Jamaica was when I was six years old, but only at the age of forty did I come to understand the meaning of it. We returned from a holiday event. It was a Good Friday event. Ma and some friends took me with them. I don't recall my sisters being there. It was like an open outdoor stadium. It is not clear, but I recall singing, dancing, and talking about God. I recall there were a lot of vendors. I remember wanting a roti because someone next to me was eating it and carrying on about how good it tasted. I remember Ma saying she did not have any money to buy anything. I was hungry, and the smell of the curry and all the other food made me more hungry.

When we got home, it was just turning dusk. I remember staying in the yard by myself. Our gate was always locked, so we were safe in the yard without supervision. With a stretched-out arm to the sky, I asked, "God, who are you?" The image of Jesus came to my mind, the same image that I saw at the event! But I kept asking and stretching my hand toward the darkening sky, asking, "Who are you? Who are you!"

I spent my whole life searching for God in the wrong places! The physical hunger I experienced at the event is parallel to the spiritual hunger I have in my heart! Only now am I being fed! That incident is my first memory of His calling and my seeking of Him.

That day, October 9, 1981, was amazing. The love we received from the neighbors when we were leaving to go to America still rests in my heart. My dad's friend picked us up to take us to the airport. Everyone in every house on the block looked out of their windows and waved goodbye to us. It was like being on a parade float and watching everyone wave to us.

On the plane, my mom had to hold Kimone in her lap because she was only one year old and didn't have a seat. I remember my mother struggling with us. Just imagine a 110 pounds lady with four little girls aged one, six, seven, and ten on an airplane for the first time!

Kimone cried the entire plane ride. By the time we were about to land, Ma was soaking wet from Kimone's urine because she did not have Pampers for her to wear. We couldn't believe the skyline upon landing. The lights and many buildings were such a beauty to behold. Our lives were about to change like never before.

CHAPTER 2

The Foundation

IT'S BEEN SAID that when one goes through therapy, the counselor's role is to get his client to exude the root of his issues and help the client navigate his own healing. Oftentimes, the root of our issues and the way we respond stem from childhood experiences and trauma. Based on my own experience, I know my childhood shaped how I felt about myself, the motivation behind my aspirations, and how I responded to and behaved in my relationships. My childhood set the foundation for a lot of the issues I faced and how I responded to them.

Our first night in America was strange. We were taken to our house, an empty two-bedroom apartment in East Flatbush, Brooklyn. When we woke up the next day, there was no toothpaste or toothbrushes for us to use. I remember my parents fussing about going to the corner store. My mom was trying to tell Dad, "There's a store across the street. Can't you just go and get it?"

My dad was reluctant but eventually went. Boy, did his mood change after that. He wasn't the same jovial man who picked us up from the airport the night before, and certainly not the same Dad I knew from Jamaica. He seemed miserable since that day. It seemed like he didn't know us. He was distant and didn't say much. Over the years, we learned that Dad didn't do much talking unless he was around his friends, specifically those he knew from Jamaica or when he was under the liquor. Up until adult age, the only time he really talked to us was to scold us. It took deep reflection to understand why Dad behaved the way he did. Of course, his childhood had a significant role in his emotional development and the reasons behind his behavior!

Denise and I started elementary school and Ingrid, junior high school. Kimone went to my grandmother, Dad's mother, who babysat for a living and lived across the street from us. Denise and I were held back. It was customary to hold back immigrant children whether from English or non-English-speaking countries. Except for my sister Ingrid because she was a walking encyclopedia. I was placed in first grade instead of second grade. It worked out best for me because I did not know how to read. At first, my classmates would laugh at me because my accent was so heavy, but in three months, I lost my accent and only pronounced a few words the Jamaican way. I learned to read quickly and excelled. School became very easy for me. I was good at reading, writing, and mathematics.

My aunt, Dad's older sister, owned a daycare center on the ground floor of the apartment building across the street. Denise and I were after-school students at the daycare. Because everyone called her Ms. Senior, we began to call our auntie Pansy and Ms. Senior as well. She was and still is a very influential and instrumental person in my life. Many blessings came to us through our close relationship with her. She would take Denise and me home with her on Friday, and we would return early Monday morning before school.

Ms. Senior lived in Uniondale, Long Island. She was one of the few black families that lived in that area since the early seventies. She traveled to Brooklyn to open and run her daycare center. It wasn't just any daycare. Ms. Senior had a master's degree in education and really taught the children under her care. Her husband, Uncle Logan, was a successful engineer and architect. Going to Long Island on the weekends gave us a snippet of what life could be like when one has an education. I quickly learned that to be successful and live a secure life, I must get a higher education.

Obtaining a higher education removes some of the obstacles that keep us in the bondage of poverty!

We were poor. All our friends who were mostly immigrants were poor as well. Our parents were fortunate enough to migrate here and took on one, sometimes two, or three jobs just to make ends meet. Our parents struggled and made just enough to pay the bills and provide for our basic needs. There were never any birthday parties or presents, getting fast food, or named brand clothing. Hand-me-down clothing was the norm. But when we visited Ms. Senior on the weekends, things were different. On our way there, she would ask us what we wanted, McDonald's or pizza. We not only got fast food, but we even had choices! When we arrived for the weekend, there was plenty of cereal to choose from, not the usual corn flakes my mom always bought. There was a variety of juice and an assortment of cookies, cakes, and ice cream. And of course, my uncle would prepare the traditional Jamaican breakfast of fried dumplings. It was like heaven. There was a huge backyard with a hammock that we napped in whether in winter or summer and a massive basement with a bedroom, bathroom, and television area. I saw the contrast between living an impoverished life in a cramped two-bedroom apartment in Brooklyn to living a comfortable life in the quiet suburbs of Long Island. At an early age, my siblings and I saw that obtaining a higher education would be the catalyst for obtaining a better lifestyle.

It was a little over a year since we'd been in America. I was seven, and we had plenty of friends from school and from the daycare center. We were the after-schoolers. I was always around kids a little older than me. There was one particular boy named Mike that was an after-school kid. He was twelve years old and was very funny. He made everyone laugh all the time. He made provocative jokes. I remember him always saying to me, "I'm gonna marry you!"

Boy, was I happy to hear that. I don't know if it was because of the absence of my dad in Jamaica when I was young or the Cinderella stories I heard in first grade, all I know is that wanting to be married had become a lifelong desire.

The daycare center was on the ground floor of the apartment building where my grandmother lived upstairs in. My other aunt also had another apartment in the same building. Behind the daycare was the building's laundry room. I don't know why I followed him, but one day, Mike lured me to follow him to the laundry room. When I got there, he told me to take off all my clothes. At age seven, I knew I should not have, but when you're naïve, you don't know how to stand up for yourself and have a crush on someone who says, "I'm going to marry you." What do you do at age seven? I foolishly did as he told me. He took off his pants and tried to have intercourse with me. He tried to penetrate me, but he too was a young boy and really didn't know what the heck he was doing. He kept trying and trying, but he couldn't because he was not (what I learned years later) erect. After what seemed like ten minutes of trying, he gave up. We went back to the daycare and continued playing like nothing happened. Then he told everyone, all our friends at the daycare that he had sex with me. It was supposed to be a secret. He and his friends would tease and laugh at me. He was so proud! What made matters worse for me emotionally was that he started liking someone else, the new pretty older girl named Sara! He stopped paying attention to me and began giving Sara all his attention, even telling her he was going to marry her.

That horrible experience left a brutal scar that resulted in the root of my guilt and shame, fear of rejection, low self-esteem, and mistrust of people, specifically men. That experience was the foundation for how I handled my relationships as a teenager, young adult in my twenties, thirties, and even early forties until the intervention and until the call that changed everything!

This calling enabled me to check, correct, and create a new foundation!

Months passed and I forgot about that encounter because Mike ran away from home and no one ever heard from him or his family again. It was said he had issues with his parents because they were strict Muslims, and he wanted to celebrate holidays with his non-Muslim friends, so he ran away.

My aunt's daycare center was a blessing for not just her immediate family but the entire neighborhood. Parents were comfortable that there was a place to leave their children and the cost was very affordable. It was a great blessing for my sisters and me because we worked there and got paid. My sister Ingrid was in high school at the time. She was responsible for cleaning the daycare after it closed. Cleaning included wiping down the tables, disinfecting the bathroom and kitchen, and sweeping and mopping the floors. My aunt threw a partner or *susu* hand, and Ingrid would get an entire draw. A partner or susu is a savings method without using the bank system. Basically, a set amount of people give one person (the collector) a set amount of money every week. Each week, a different person from the group keeps the lump sum. For example, ten people decide to give the collector (the one who collects weekly) $100 every week for ten weeks. Each week a different person keeps the $1,000 total that is collected. This would be done every week for ten consecutive weeks because there are ten different people involved. This is how many immigrant families are able to save money quickly. Some people would be in $5,000 or higher partners.

Ingrid was smart. She hired our best friend at the time, Denise, and me to help her clean. When Ingrid got her partner hand, which was about $1,200, she would split it among us.

Working at the daycare gave us the money we needed to buy the clothes we wanted, makeup, have hair salon treatments once in a while, and of course, buy the latest sneakers that everyone else wore. Most importantly, working at such a young age instilled the ethics of working hard to get what we wanted for ourselves.

When Andrew was born in 1986, I became the middle child at home. We also have older siblings from my dad's side who lived in Jamaica, and to my understanding, Dad was preparing paperwork for them to migrate to America as well.

At age ten, I was very mature and kept out of trouble. Ma's left hand is heavy beyond understanding despite her small-sized body. At first, Dad didn't hit us too much. I avoided any possible trouble, so occasionally, he would conk me on my forehead but not too often. One time, I went to my friend's birthday party in the apartment adjacent to my grandmother's apartment. Grandma's apartment was 7D, and the party was held at apartment 7C, whose building was across the street. I came back from the party just before 7:00 p.m., before it got dark. All I know is that the conk on my forehead was so painful, I was surprised I did not pass out. So I learned very quickly to do as they say, overextend myself, and avoid getting licks (Jamaican term for a whipping) from my parents. I became very independent and tried to be helpful around the house.

I can't explain where Denise, Ingrid, or Kimone were. Dad was most likely at work, driving his cab. Ma must have been at work too. I was left at home alone and the super (building janitor) was scheduled to come and fix the leaking pipe under our kitchen sink. We lived in a community of four apartment buildings that were managed by the same management company. Each building had one or two supers, but for some jobs, the supers would cross and exchange buildings, depending on the repair needed.

The families in these buildings knew all the supers and mostly each other! We were mostly immigrant families from Africa and various Caribbean islands with similar migration stories. Just about everyone looked out for each other. Neighbors would keep an eye on us as we played double Dutch all day. It was like my friends' parents were also our parents. They were able to correct us if they saw or heard anyone of us misbehaving outside. And we could be sure our mother would hear about it. In fact, everyone called each other by their first and last names. That was the culture of our community.

I opened the door, and it was Larry, the super for one of the other buildings. He came to fix the pipe. I led him to the kitchen and showed him under the sink. Apparently, he figured out I was home alone. I stayed in the kitchen as he was fixing the pipe. Who would have thought laughing Larry was a monster! After fixing the pipe for about ten minutes, he turned to me and lifted up my shirt. He took his nasty greasy oiled-up hand and began touching my breast.

I yelled, "Stop it" and pulled down my shirt. He attempted to do it again, but I screamed, "No!"

Then he said, "I'm not finished. I have to come back next week to finish the work." He walked to the door and let himself out, and I locked it. I knew that he would never find me home by myself the next week. I never told Ma because she would have created World War III, and I thought she would have brought more embarrassment to the issue. She certainly would have called the police.

Ma doesn't hold her tongue when she is upset. When we first moved to America and were adjusting to having new friends at my aunt's daycare center, she came to the daycare center with the belt to beat us because we didn't do our chores or something. Ms. Senior, my aunt, and her sister-in-law had to hold her back and remind her that we are not in Jamaica and tell her she can't do that here. So I thought telling Ma about what Larry did would have caused a big embarrassing scene. Telling Dad would mean death for Larry and jail for Dad.

Dad didn't talk to us much; but he was very, very protective of us, his daughters. We came to that conclusion when Denise had a male friend she would play with in the lobby of our building. One day, Dad came home and saw them running around the lobby. Dad beat him left and right and kept kicking him in his behind, just for playing with Denise. In that same time period, Ma, Dad, and Ingrid went to visit one of his friends. Dad's friend had a son! Ingrid was about thirteen or fourteen, and the son was around the same age. All Ingrid and the son did was talk in the corner, perhaps they were too friendly for Dad's taste. That was enough to enrage Dad because they came back from their visit early. Ma said Dad made such a scene with the boy by either hitting him and certainly cussing him out that they had to leave, and Dad lost his friendship with the boy's father.

In retrospect, I realized Dad had a lot of children with various women, which was condoned culturally back then. Perhaps because of Dad's own behavior toward women or that was his way to express his love for us, he was extremely protective of his daughters. I was too embarrassed and ashamed to tell anyone what Larry the super did.

About a year later, we heard that Larry's wife passed away from cancer, breast cancer! For years, I wondered and was bothered about her passing. Despite what he did, I strangely felt terribly sad for him. After his wife's passing, he never walked around laughing and was certainly no longer laughing Larry. His hair turned gray quickly. I wondered if she already had cancer when he touched me or if her cancer was his punishment for touching me, a ten-year-old. It is not my place to figure that out. Nor do I want to think that an innocent woman would suffer because of her husband. However, after the call, I begin to learn about the promises of God.

**God is just: He will pay back trouble to those who trouble you.
—2 Thessalonians 1:6 New International Version (NIV)**

That same summer, when I was ten, I spent the entire summer helping Grandma babysit the babies under one year old. I would change their Pampers, heat up their food, and help them go to sleep. I hated the job! I did not get to go to the park or on any of the trips with the daycare center that summer because I was busy helping grandma from 8:00 a.m. to 6:00 p.m. I was glad to get the $20 per week though. I saved every penny and, at the end of the summer, was able to buy myself back-to-school clothes and a real not the fake, pair of Reeboks. I went back to school (fifth grade) looking fly as ever because I didn't have on as many hand-me-down clothes or the fake Reeboks. I had the real thing!

I kept working at the daycare center until it closed around 1988. The building managers gave my aunt a difficult time renewing her lease, so she closed the daycare and began teaching elementary school children at the New York City Board of Education.

Since the daycare closed, there were three kids from the daycare who did not have anywhere to go after school. Since I was in eighth grade and got home before they left elementary school, I became their after-school sitter. I charged their mothers $15 per week. Every week, I made $45 to watch three kids from 3:00 p.m. to 6:00 p.m.

Ma was happy. This $45 covered the television we finally bought for our room and the cable bill and the occasional Chinese food or Domino's Pizza we would order. I was always blessed financially. I always worked since a young age. God always made a way!

When I graduated from junior high school, I got accepted to Murry Bergtraum High School in Manhattan. It was the summer of 1989. I attempted to join the summer youth employment program through my junior high school in Brooklyn. The sign-up process was crazy. It seemed like every teenager in Brooklyn was on the line to get a summer job. Upon joining the line that extended around the block, I waited for about four hours in the midst of shouting, pushing, shoving, and cursing only to learn that there was no guarantee of getting a placement. Also, in sixth and seventh grade, I was loud and boisterous like some of my friends that were in the line. But there was a shift in me internally.

While waiting in line, I started to feel out of place and uncomfortable. I was very quiet that day, not wanting to engage in any conversation. My friends kept asking if I was okay. I would say, "Yeah, I'm fine " but kept quiet. In retrospect, I think the Lord was already starting the work of separation. I took a leap of faith and suddenly left the line after four hours of waiting to inquire at my soon-to-be high school in Manhattan. It is sad to say, but back then, a high school in Manhattan near the financial district was a different environment and a better opportunity.

When I visited my high school to sign up for the summer youth employment program the next day, there was no line! I took classes for three weeks and then worked for three weeks. The job placement was held at a special location (another high school) where we got to choose from a number of city agencies where we wanted to work. I was debating whether to sign up to work at One Police Plaza (the headquarters for NYPD), which was directly across the street from my soon-to-be high school, or sign up to work at Health and Hospitals Corporation headquarters, which is a few blocks from my soon-to-be high school. I chose New York City Health and Hospitals Corporation (HHC), thinking I would be placed at a hospital. They placed me in the office of Ambulatory Care Services.

I worked there for three weeks, just making copies and answering the phone. I did not know the hand of God yet, but God sure knew me.

> **Before I formed you in the womb I knew you,**
> **before you were born I set you apart.**
> **—Jeremiah 1:5 NIV**

Here comes the unexpected blessing. The human resources department needed an intern all year long and my friend who worked in the office next door was hired to stay on after the SYEP program ended. After I finished my three weeks of summer youth employment in the Ambulatory Care Services office, guess where I was hired! The human resources department. My friend told them about me, and the rest was history. I was on their payroll as a permanent intern. What a magnificent blessing. I went from waiting in line for at least four hours in Brooklyn, hoping to get placement to work three weeks over the summer, to being placed in an office at the headquarters for HHC to being hired permanently in the human resources department all year long and summers.

My schedule was conveniently arranged so that I left school at 2:00 p.m. I was able to work every day from 2:00 p.m. to 5:00 p.m. How wonderful getting paid the minimum wage of $3.25 an hour, fifteen hours per week. During the next four summers to come, I did not need to work as an SYEP student because I was already their regular intern, so I worked Monday through Friday from 9:00 to 5:00 p.m. during the summer months. The income enabled me to not ask Ma and Dad for anything! It was a blessing for me but a greater one for them: one less child to worry about feeding and clothing.

My employment at HHC set the foundation for my employment to this day. Since 1989, at the age of fourteen, I have been on the New York City payroll and was only transferred a few times from one city agency to another but never left the system. Working at HHC set the foundation for my blessings and trials in employment at a young age!

By my senior year of high school, I moved out. Yes, at age seventeen, I was living with Ingrid, who was twenty-one years old. Since I started working on the books and always had a little bit of extra money, my dream was to move out as soon as possible. I didn't think I would make it to eighteen years old living with Ma, Dad, Denise, Kimone, and my younger brother, Andrew. The two-bedroom apartment was cramped. Dad's drinking was not getting any better; actually, it was unbearable. In retrospect, Andrew was young, so he didn't really experience the harsh discipline from Dad when he was under the liquor like Ingrid, Denise, Kimone, and I did when we were his age. However, Denise and Kimone were left behind and had to deal with it. It could not have been easy for them. I always felt bad that Ingrid and I were able to escape the chaos but they were left behind.

My aunt and uncle had a one-bedroom apartment across the street from where we lived. They bought a house in North Carolina and moved in the summer of 1992. So Ingrid was able to take over the apartment, and I moved in with her. I used my savings to partition the living room and create a bedroom for myself. Those were the years of fun, freedom, and party.

We would have fish fry Fridays. All our friends, especially those from Long Island, would come over and Ingrid would fry fish, and we would stay up and watch subtitled kung fu movies. The 45 (Colt 45) and blunt certainly circulated. Ingrid and I danced for a house singer; we were her exclusive backup dancers. We traveled the club scene throughout the city. We would hold show rehearsals, jam sessions, and ongoing parties in our apartment. Ingrid and I were exposed to a lot of weed smoking and alcohol, but we definitely didn't drink. After witnessing our dad's irrational behavior when he drank excessively, we did not touch the bottle. And we certainly tried to avoid dating guys who drank heavily. Drinking was the deal breaker in my dating life. I had asthma, so I was afraid to smoke the blunt that was passed around even though they tried to encourage me that the ganja (Jamaican term for marijuana) would be good for my asthma.

Our apartment became the unofficial club scene, recording studio, and talent showcase place. I kept red fluorescent lights in my room at all times, and Ingrid had blue lights. On my bedroom side of the wall that separated my bedroom room from our living room was a huge mural with the words "Lady Miss Tee!" In retrospect, I thought I was so hot and I was so vain! Anyone who step foot in our apartment to hang out had to have a raw talent and had to tag their name on the wall. So many people and so much talent came through. My boyfriend at the time was a DJ and had his DJ equipment and crates of records set up in our living room. We played music seven days a week. My sister's friend was a rapper and singer. They would create tracks in the studio but come to our apartment to write and rehearse their lyrics. The lady whom we danced for had a son who was an aspiring rapper! He moved in, and the music and noise were endless.

I was still in high school and worked after school. Every Wednesday, we were at one particular club, partying until 4:00 a.m. I still made it to school and kept up my grades. Our apartment was on the seventh floor, and all our neighbors on our floor loved us. They understood us. It was like Saturday night at the Apollo, so when we didn't make music, they were concerned and inquired. They said we entertained them. We had the house music crew that would come through. Then, the dancehall crew mixed with the hip-hop crew would visit.

Those years were one of the most festive days of my life. I don't ever remember us being tired. I partied during the week and all weekend and went to school and work on time. It seemed like a wildlife because Ingrid and I were exposed to drugs from some of the club scenes we frequented, but we were never coerced or encouraged to use any. It was there in abundance, in our faces, but there must have been divine protection on us. We were near it, but never used it!

Everything changed when an older couple moved downstairs from us. They didn't understand that we were young and just harmlessly having fun. They complained about the noise. They wrote letters to the management about us. They tried to get the neighbors to also complain about us. It got so bad that they would use their broom to bang on their ceiling just to silence the noise we created. They won their petition because our lease was not renewed for the following year. The management claimed it was due to our excessive noise.

I had already graduated from high school and was trying to figure out how I was going to pay for my college tuition. In my first year of college, I attended New York City Technical College and was able to pay my own tuition, but things looked difficult in planning for the next year. I couldn't claim independence because I was under the age of twenty-three or twenty-six. There was some kind of new law that stated you had to be over a certain age to claim independence regardless of your living situation. I was only nineteen years old, so I didn't meet the age requirement. My parents claimed me even though I lived on my own. The law didn't allow me to claim myself because of my age.

I was angry. How is that fair? I can prove my independence, I thought! But it didn't matter because my parents had already claimed me even if I would have been of age. I was livid! But again, I didn't know it, at the time, but God had a different plan. He had a better plan. When God calls us, he calls us into His marvelous plan for our lives. He tells us in Jeremiah 29:11 NIV: **"For I know the plans I have for you, declares the Lord, plans to prosper you and not to harm you, plans to give you hope and a future."**

If I had known this and understood this at that time, I would not have spent so much time in resentment, angry at my parents and the government for what I thought was a hindrance to getting a higher education.

I was still working at Health and Hospitals Corporation. The director of human resources had left to become the director of human resources at Hunter College the year before. I remember telling my colleague that I didn't know how I was going to pay for my tuition and that I need another job. He kept in touch with Carl Haynes, the gentleman who used to be our director of human resources at HHC (Health and Hospitals Corporation). He called him right there on the spot and asked if there were any openings at Hunter College because I was looking for full-time work. Mr. Haynes told him, "I remember that young lady, Tee! She was very nice. Send her to my office!"

I was shocked because I was just a high school student who worked after school and always stayed out of the big shots' (directors) way. I didn't think that he would remember me. I arrived at Hunter College. He told me that he knew I was qualified, but I still would need to take and pass a typing test of forty words per minute to be hired for the full-time position. Little did he know, I took typing in high school and already typed ninety words per minute. I was hired and was the youngest full-time employee, an office associate, at Hunter College at that time.

Working at Hunter College, which is a CUNY (City University of New York) school, was a great blessing beyond understanding. I was able to attend any of the CUNY colleges for free after six months of employment. I worked at Hunter College full-time during the day and attended school in the evening and on weekends for free! I only had to pay an activity fee of about $56 per semester. God has always been so good to me even when I didn't know Him. I worked at Hunter College from 1994–1999, exactly five years until I graduated from college. It was also five years that I needed to be vested in the pension plan, which enabled me to leave with some level of financial security. The timing was perfect!

Just before leaving Hunter College, I started shifting into a different person. At around the age of twenty, when I was living by myself entirely, I knew there was a drastic shift. I would still go to a few parties and, once in a while, go clubbing, but it felt awkward. I didn't want to be there. I had no interest in partying anymore. At first, I was going with my friends to please them but then stopped joining them. The few parties that I attended with them, I felt out of place. No one noticed the shift, but I did. It was an internal shift. I started to become shy and more timid around others on the job or anywhere except for when I was around my very close friends and family. I hated to speak publicly and certainly became an extreme introvert. The public speaking issue was so real that I was able to dodge speech class, which is supposed to be a requirement in college. To this day, I don't know how I dodged speech or what class I took to substitute it. All I know is I obtained a bachelor's degree and two separate master's degrees but never took speech! It's only by the grace of God!

The thing we run from the most is often the thing we end up running into, especially when it is connected to our divine purpose!

In June 1999, after six long years of work and study, I finally graduated from college. It was such a great feeling to accomplish one of my lifelong goals. I was the first one in my immediate family to graduate with a bachelor's. I applied for graduate school in pursuit of becoming a social worker. I started my first graduate semester at Fordham University's school of social work. I was hoping to get into Hunter College's Silberman School of Social Work, which would have cost me nothing because it is a CUNY school but was rejected. I took out a loan to attend the expensive-as-ever Fordham University, a private college although I still worked for CUNY.

Hunter College Human Resources (my department) had an opening for an assistant director position. I just got the degree and knew that I was more than qualified for the position. They even interviewed me for the position first. However, someone else was hired, an outsider. I did not appreciate that I was basically doing the job and understood it from already working in the office, yet they allowed me to go through the interviewing process but had someone else in mind for the position. Disappointed, depressed, and embarrassed were just some of my sentiments about the whole deceptive process. Again, I did not know that the hand of God was on me, so I didn't understand yet that any rejection is really God's protection and redirection for his plans for my life.

Soon after, I was so glad that I did not get hired in that position! I would have probably gotten comfortable and dropped out of graduate school and certainly would not have been working in the areas of my passions, which are teaching and doing social work! I quickly learned that, sometimes, the door has to close for another one to open. Sometimes the door gets slammed in our faces, and it hurts. When I look over my life and recall all the slammed doors and rejections, I see how it had to be that way, and it worked out for my good.

And we know that in all things, God works for the good of those who love him, who have been called according to His purpose.
                                                      —Romans 8:28 NIV

Sometimes we walk through doors that we have no business entering, and then we pray that God would open them and rescue us! It's just better to appreciate the slammed doors!

When I was going to the daycare at around age ten, I would gather a few of the younger children and pretend to be their teacher. Teaching was plan B, and becoming a social worker was plan A. I like the thought of helping others. I wanted to serve and thought social work was the best career for me. But while at Fordham University Graduate School of Social Service, my colleague at Hunter College, who also graduated and wanted to leave, got a teaching job. She told me about the need for teachers throughout the city and encouraged me to apply at 65 Court Street, the department of education headquarters. In fact, she began her teaching career in September but continued to work at Hunter College part-time in the evening. She was chasing money. I remember her stopping by human resources every single day to provoke me. "You still here! You got a degree, and you still here!" she would say. "Go down to the board of education with your transcript and they will evaluate and hire you right away."

I had already taken the LAST (Liberal Arts and Sciences Test) teacher's examination and passed in preparation for my plan B, which was becoming a teacher. The board of education sent me to a hiring pool for district 14. I had no idea about district 14 and didn't know that it was considered a difficult-to-fill vacancy area. When I got there, one of the prospective teachers was walking and complaining loudly, "I ain't working in no bad neighborhood! They only have openings in those bad schools in the worst neighborhoods," while shaking her head as she exited, and I entered.

The interview process was very comical. I was led into a huge room with about thirty other applicants. I was not dressed for an interview like the other candidates. Many had on business suits and briefcases. I had on biker boots, a regular long skirt, and a button-down blouse. I was sitting in the room, nonchalant about getting called for a one-on-one interview. I was busy flipping through my *People*'s gossip magazine just to pass the time.

An older gentleman came into the room, approached me, and asked me to follow him to another area where I would be interviewed. He asked me three questions: "Do you want to work in district 14? Are you ready to work right away? And if your answer is yes, can you come to the school to meet the principal because he would need to meet you and give his approval?"

My answer was yes, yes, and yes, but I don't have a car and where is this school anyway. In ten minutes, I found myself in my soon-to-be new supervisor's car, going to the school, which became my place of employment for the next nine or so years.

The principal was not impressed with the assistant principal's choice of hiring me because I was shy and didn't say much. After glancing over my resume, he said, "I see you have no teaching experience. Do you think you could handle the children in this community?" I said yes although I didn't know much about the community. The school is located on the borderline of Bushwick, Bedford-Stuyvesant, and Williamsburg. It was considered a super hotspot for drugs and high crime. I'm from East Flatbush and lived in Sunset Park briefly. At that time, I knew nothing about the reality of living in or around Bedford-Stuyvesant/Bushwick, and gentrification, which propels more police presence, had not started yet! My preconceived notion about the community was very negative, but I was determined to handle it. Life could be so paradoxical. That neighborhood that I thought would have been problematic because of the poverty and high crime was actually a blessing for me. The school is situated in the middle of Tompkins's housing projects. The Sumner projects are next to the school and Marcy Projects is right down the block. I developed fond feelings for my school community, my colleagues, and my students. I loved even on the weekends visiting the neighborhood to get Chinese food and Spanish food from the Dominican restaurant down the block from my school. It was also a joy to drive by and see my students outside the school building over the weekend. There was something special about working in the hood!

The principal warmed up when I told him I took a lot of history classes because he was a history major in college. But overall, he wasn't impressed and said, "I guess they don't have anyone more qualified willing to come here!"

I wanted to say, "I heard that," but appreciate his frankness. My supervisor, the assistant principal, who pulled me from the hiring pool, became a very great support to me during my first year, which was difficult, to say the least.

Years later, I asked him why he picked me out of all the individuals who were there. He just bypassed everyone and asked me to come with him for an interview. He said he could tell that some of the candidates most likely would not stay. I had just turned twenty-five years old and was one of the youngest candidates in the room. I believe that might have had something to do with it. Or was it God's favor that has always been prevalent even though I did not know Him as of yet?

He was right though about handling our students; it was not easy. In the teaching profession, you either have it or you don't have it. If your heart is not there, you will not make it. It can't be about the money, because the money isn't a lot, considering the education requirements. They couldn't pay us enough for the number of hats that we wear as teachers. To be a good and effective teacher, we have to go beyond instructions. We have to show them love and gain their trust first. This doesn't mean being soft and wishy-washy. Without love and trust teaching will be difficult. We must wear various hats. Sometimes, we have to just listen, play the role of counselor, and still make time to teach the mandated curriculum because students come in with so much heaviness and emotional issues. As teachers, especially in a community where our children have encountered the effects of socioeconomic injustices that cause trauma and brokenness, we must provide more than academic instruction.

My first year was difficult. I was inexperienced, and the issues that my students faced outside of school affected them inside of school. Many were in foster care, being raised by grandparents who didn't have it altogether but tried their best, and many fathers were missing or in prison. These are just some of the common issues my students faced.

I wasn't fully experienced to handle some things, but I kept on pushing because I wanted to make a difference. It was hard. I was their third teacher to take over that class my first year, and we were only in the month of November. I remember my first week of taking over the class, one of my students said, "You not gonna stay 'cause we bad, we *real* bad!" I made a decision that I was going to stay and do my best. I was not going to quit no matter what. And they were not bad at all; they were very behind academically. Yes, I broke up a few fights here and there. My supervisor would always say, "You're in the trenches. Just make it out." It took time, but eventually, I found my niche. I wasn't a strong disciplinarian like my friend and mentor teacher, Ms. Williams-Jones. I couldn't be like other experienced teachers because I simply didn't have that kind of experience yet. However, I developed a reward system and used it until they gained my trust. It got so simple that I didn't need the reward system anymore. It took three years to fully understand good and effective classroom management.

I was assigned to the library and worked as the library teacher (not a certified librarian yet). The classes that were more challenging with behavior issues participated in plays aligned to stories, poetry reading and writing, and a lot of research projects with oral presentations. We had our own little show and tell, onstage plays, and storytelling contests that kept them engaged in reading, writing, speaking, and listening, which was one of the NYS ELA (English Language Arts) standards. They loved it and so did I.

In one particular fifth-grade class, I had difficulty getting them to stay engaged. I had a hard time getting them to focus on research or read aloud. Some of them were struggling readers way below their grade level. I found book sets that were made into movies. For that particular class, I allowed them to watch the movie first, knowing they would enjoy it, and then use it as a motivation to read the actual book. They thought they would escape reading by watching the movie. Ha! Normally, teachers would assign the book first and then the movie as a follow-up. But that's what it took to get them motivated to read and write consistently. It worked; they were writing to compare and contrast the movie to the book. They started to ask about other books that were converted into a movie. Once they got comfortable with comparing and contrasting movies to book versions, I switched it up on them and started having them read the books first then followed up with the movie version! Then I weaned them off reading book sets that had a movie version and just chose interesting chapter books similar to the ones they watched. Mission accomplished! My students in that class were reading with enthusiasm! As teachers, many times, we have to go outside of the box to accomplish our goals. Sometimes we have to do whatever means necessary!

It was Black History Month 2005. I wanted some students to participate in the great Black History Month assembly Ms. Williams-Jones would always produce. Because there was very little time to rehearse something lengthy, I chose ten students to read facts about Dr. King's life. Each student had to read two sentences. As I was preparing the sentences on an index card, something said (I didn't know the voice of God yet), but something told me, Why not make the sentences rhyme? It would be a better presentation. After a few minutes of playing with the wording, I had a poem in my hand. That was the foundation for writing poems. My principal posted it in one of her monthly newsletters, which encouraged me to write another poem the following year for Black History Month. I also wrote a poem about Malcolm X and had our students read it.

This was the birth of my poetry writing. It all began with just putting words together for an elementary school assembly. Who would have thought that, years later, my inception to preaching started when I wrote and recited a poem for my pastor's anniversary? Life is a puzzle, and God puts the pieces together to create a masterpiece as we journey through it! Below are the two school poems written for children for the Black History Month assembly. A few verses were modified in 2015 to be used in church with my Sunday school children.

Remembering Dr. King

"I have a Dream" is a very great speech
However, Dr. Martin Luther King Jr. did many more things

He was part of the *Boycott the Bus* movement
As a result, there was some improvement
In the lives of Black people and others
Look around, see, we are all sisters and brothers

He fought for freedom and equality
Regardless of race, religion, and creed

He marched in the hot sun
And sat in jail to fulfill an equal rights need

It is important to know
Dr. King did not do this alone
White people joined him too
It seems some had the same dream
Dr. Martin Luther King Jr. was also a minister
He believed in education
And was against violence and segregation
Segregation means Blacks and Whites can't live
And do things together
Thanks to his hard work,
We're allowed to live wherever
Dr. King's faith in God was so strong
It was his faith that gave him the strength
to fight against
Those laws that were so wrong
Dr. Martin Luther King Jr. won the 1964 Nobel Peace Prize
For bringing peace and equality to our lives
Unfortunately, a man who did not know about love but only hate
Shot and killed Dr. King in 1968
Today people all around the world remember him and celebrate
All the things he has done for us
My God he was great!

2005

<u>The Truth about Malcolm X</u>

Malcolm Little was born in 1925
His father died
His mother got sick
So he became a foster child
As a teenager, he became a hustler
A street boy who dropped out of school

A robber and a gambler too
Eventually, he went to jail for his crimes
It took some time before he realized
There is another way to life
He was introduced to *The Nation of Islam* Religion
Under the leadership of Elijah Muhammad
He changed his name from Malcolm Little to Malcolm X
At that time he thought dropping his "slave" name was best
He started working real hard and began to preach
"By Any Means Necessary" for blacks to have equality
This was different from Dr. King's non-violence strategy
But he made a religious trip to Mecca
It changed his life forever
For the first time he saw people of all races praying together
He changed his name again from Malcolm X to
Malik El Hajj Shabazz and left
The Nation of Islam religion
Then took the next step
He became an advocate for
Peace and human rights
To all brothers and sisters alike
This makes me wonder
Had he lived a little longer
Would he have converted to the
Preaching and teachings of Jesus
It's something to think about
For he was in the middle of a spiritual transformation
That transcended way beyond the issues of this nation
But unfortunately
His changing of religion cost him his life
He left behind four children and a pregnant wife

2006

CHAPTER 3

From the Outside

I WAS DOING VERY well, working as a teacher, and had completed my master's degree in education. I bought a brand-new car and traveled a bit to Jamaica, London, and Paris, and pretty much things seem to be going well according to the plans on my mental check-off list. From the outside, everything looked great! But on the inside, I struggled. I struggled with insecurity and low self-esteem. I struggled with depression and anxiety, but it was and had to be hidden.

One of my sisters was already diagnosed with manic depression and schizophrenia. This mental illness is no joke! The symptoms of schizophrenia often include violence, hallucination, suicide attempts, and alcohol, addiction. Thank God my mother has a strong grip on my sister and makes sure that she takes her medicine. With my sister's well-known mental illness, there was no way I could reveal my hidden depression. It would have been too much, not to mention my mom was still handling my dad's drinking issue. Also, Ingrid and I were seen as the strong ones, so disclosure of any possible mental issue on my end would have probably sent my mother over the edge, or so I thought. So I suffered in silence. From the outside, everything appeared to be well!

I dated here and there, but my last boyfriend, who was a good childhood friend, had a serious drinking problem. The last straw was on New Year's Eve when Ingrid, another childhood friend, and I went to see one of our favorite bands, in which V. Jeffrey Smith, from the group The Family Stand, was going to perform. The most amazing way to celebrate New Year's Eve, right?

My boyfriend entered the small venue with a big bouquet of flowers for me. He greeted me with a huge hug and kiss. Everyone in the venue was impressed; they were tapping him on the shoulder for his grand gesture of love on New Year's Eve. A dude that was behind us joked and yelled, "That's right! Chivalry still exists!" Thirty minutes into the night, he started acting weird. He kept circling the venue, hugging people inappropriately, and wouldn't sit down. What started off as a wonderful impressive gesture became a great embarrassment! Ingrid kept asking, "Where is he?"

I kept saying, "You know. He must be at the bar."

By the time I turned around to look by the bar, he was in his wife beater (the white undergarment men wear under their shirts). I was like, "Ingrid, I know he didn't just take off his shirt in here!" It was a very cold New Year's Eve, probably 10 degrees or lower. By the end of the night, better yet, we didn't stay for the entire show to see the end of the night. We ended up dragging him out of the club because he was trying to take off all his clothes. Lord have mercy! It was so difficult getting him to the car. He began throwing up as I started to drive. What a way to bring in the New Year. It was not unusual that he would drink and get a little drunk, but this New Year's Eve incident was on a whole different level. I didn't know how serious and deep his drinking addiction was. We dated on and off for a year, and I didn't see him often, so I didn't really know the extent of his drinking. However, in the few outings that we attended, we would leave with him getting drunk. How on Earth did I overlook that? I learned that he would drink at least half a dozen of beers before we reached the event so that, by the time we got to our destination and after the addition of hard liquor, he transformed into an insulting drunk. I wanted to break up with him long before that New Year's Eve disaster but didn't. My family loved him because we knew him for years, and he was charming and nice when he wasn't drunk. However, that New Year's Eve night was the last straw!

I dropped him home and knew that we were done. I cared about him especially since he was my cousin's close friend and we knew each other since I was fifteen years old. He was one of the guys that use to come over during our fish fry Fridays like ten years before. But I had enough of his behavior of drinking and drunkenness, which was the deal breaker. The next day, January 1, I went back to his house to pick up some personal items. His mother opened the door. She told me he was sleeping but to go take a look at him. He had a huge knot in the middle of his forehead. Apparently, he fell off his bed and hit his head. He woke up and didn't remember falling. I told him we were done! I pray that he is alive and well! After my break up with him, I didn't date for a long time.

I started to work on myself physically when really it was my emotional state that needed more attention. I started to work out a lot and changed my diet. This was the time when South Beach (thanks to Hilary Clinton) and the Atkins diet were popular. I was always a vegetarian since age thirteen but began the famous Atkins diet. I lost a lot of weight, being a vegetarian, and following the Atkins diet. I lost almost 50 pounds and kept it off for almost three years until I had my daughter. I went from size 14 to size 8 and stayed there. The Atkins diet consists of high protein, mostly meat with very little carbohydrates. How on earth did I eat a diet that consisted of high protein such as meat when I was a vegetarian? Atkins and vegetarian are like oil to water. I did it though. But then, during that time, I would have spells of racing heartbeat!

The racing heartbeat went on and off for weeks. The weeks turned into months. I didn't tell anyone! It got worse and worse that I would pull over while driving because I would feel like I was going to lose control of the wheels and thought I was having a heart attack. I thought it was my diet of high protein but soon learned otherwise.

Many times, I would rub my wrist in public in front of my students but I was secretly checking my pulse. No one knew what I was feeling on the inside or could have recognized my habit of rubbing my wrist. And, of course, from the outside, my life seemed to be in order. There were times when I would feel pain in my abdomen. I would literally feel a throbbing pain on my side! I would go to the emergency room because I experienced chest pain. Sure enough, they would take my pressure and run an EKG and send me home! "You're healthy, besides your heart rate being a bit fast, you have a perfect blood pressure rate of 120 over 80. Your EKG is normal." This would go on week after week. First the chest pain, then the emergency room, and then the result, showing that I'm healthy.

One day, I was driving with my friend Karen to the mall. The chest pain started. I pulled over in the parking lot before parking the car correctly, jumped out of the car, and started to scream, "I'm having a heart attack. My chest, my chest."

Poor Karen. She must have been frightened. We both called the ambulance. On my cell phone, I said, "Come quickly. I'm having a heart attack!"

As they approached me, I noticed they were not rushing. The paramedics showed up fast but then started taking their time, asking me questions, like what's my name. Then they asked me where I wanted to go and which hospital. The drive to the hospital was like a cruise; they didn't even put on the siren. They must have known that I was not having a heart attack or something because I kept telling them, "Hurry up! Get me to the hospital quickly!" But they took their time. They took me to the nearest hospital.

The emergency room was crazy and crowded. There was a wait, a long wait. I overheard a male nurse speaking with a Jamaican accent. I did not know what he looked like but remembered that my mother had a childhood friend from Jamaica who was a nurse and a pastor and worked at that hospital. I asked the nurse with the accent if he knew Pastor M. He kind of hushed me but pulled me to the side to inquire who I was. How ironic; he then told me he was indeed Pastor M. but said not to call him pastor there. Upon learning whose daughter I was, he discreetly bypassed a bunch of patients who were waiting before me and got me to the examination room immediately. Once again, the EKG showed no signs of heart issues except for a rapid heartbeat. They couldn't figure out why my heart was beating so fast and attributed the rapid heart rate to the usage of my asthma inhaler.

This falling out in the parking lot happened in December 2004. I spent the entire year of 2005 battling with what my primary doctor had always said was anxiety. I recall visiting my primary physician right after the parking lot incident. I would insist that I might have ovarian cancer because of the pain I felt on my side. I insisted that I was going to have a massive stroke because of the constant headache. I insisted that I had a heart condition because of the rapid heartbeat and need to catch my breath although it wasn't due to the shortness of breath from asthma. But my primary doctor kept telling me I was healthy, and it was anxiety.

The entire year of 2005 was brutal. I would go to work and come home, to the basement apartment I rented in my parent's home. I would be home by three forty-five, turn off all the lights, and try to sleep. I would experience panic attacks upon attack and more attacks then go back to sleep.

My sister Ingrid lived on the third floor, in the rental unit of the family house. She would come downstairs and try something called Reiki. Reiki is supposed to be a healing technique, a Japanese energy transformation for healing. It was a form of massage therapy. It worked temporarily, but the minute Ingrid left my room, the rapid heartbeat and the feeling like I was going to pass out would come back.

It took about five months, around the spring of 2005, before I finally accepted that although I was physically healthy, I was suffering from anxiety, a mental disorder. And I did not know anything about anxiety. Some days, it got so bad, I would have strong suicidal thoughts. I never thought I had the guts to do it, nor did I plan to commit suicide; all I know was that I wanted to die. I knew I couldn't continue living like this.

Once I knew what it was, I began to research and attempted counseling. For the first time in my life, I tried psychotherapy. After three sessions of hypnosis and no results, I gave up on the therapy. I remembered three Sundays in a row I would go to Brooklyn Heights to meet my therapist in his brownstone house on the ground floor. It bothered me that he had on the same outfit three weeks in a row, and it was dirty. It bothered me that he didn't ask me about my past, like the counseling I saw on television or heard about from friends. It bothered me that he would have me lie down on the dirty couch, play some chanting-type meditative music, and hypnotize me. It bothered me that when I arrived, someone was leaving, and as I left my session, someone was entering. It bothered me that when I left there, I still felt anxious on the way home. Did he even clean the couch in between sessions? I wondered. Or was it just my OCD (obsessive-compulsive disorder) in addition to anxiety that had me overreacting? He gave me copies of the tapes he used, so I would be able to play them at home, but I was never able to hypnotize myself. The tapes calm me down temporarily though. After the tapes, I went back to experiencing the same symptoms of anxiety.

Thank God for the Internet! I began researching and reading about my condition. I learned about breathing techniques from someone online who lived all the way in England and suffered. I remember reading that I should avoid taking medication because once you get on anxiety medication, you wouldn't be able to get off it. So when the therapist suggested medication for me as an option, I didn't even respond to him.

When I would hyperventilate, I learned how to breathe it out! I continued to research and stumbled upon a program about coping with anxiety. It was the Lucinda Bassett program. I think I spent about $300 on the kit, which consisted of audio and VHS tapes (this was in 2005). I can't explain why I didn't purchase the CD version. I got way more than $300 worth of therapy. This program helped me tremendously. Using the program taught me how to breathe by inhaling slowly, holding my breath for a few seconds, and then exhaling slower than how I inhaled. I learned to ignore the sensation when it comes. The sensations were real and strong. I learned how to self-talk. The self-talk cards really came in handy. I would tell myself, "No, I'm not going to die. No, I'm not going to have a heart attack. No, I'm not going to have an aneurysm," even though I felt the symptoms physically.

Anxiety is a mental disorder. It affected me in a way that if I read about an illness, I would experience its symptoms or sensations. I learned the power of distraction. Over time, I realized that when I felt the symptoms but distracted myself by calling up someone and just talking, the symptoms would diminish. Following the Lucinda Bassett program helped me tremendously, and over time, I got better. When my heart beat fast, I ignored it. When I felt severe headaches, I ignored them. When I felt I was about to hyperventilate, I applied the breathing technique for ten minutes until I was calm again. I would breathe in front of my students; they had no idea. I would apply the breathing technique while driving and around others, but no one knew.

I suffered the entire year of 2005, but as time passed, I got better. The symptoms were still strong, but I learned to ignore them until they went away. My attacks became less frequent.

It was New Year's Day, January 1, 2006. Something always happened on New Year's Day! It has truly been a day of new beginnings. I was on the airplane with my childhood friend, Nicky, returning from vacation in Florida. I remember saying in prayer on the airplane, "God, please help me. I cannot go through another year of anxiety. I refuse to go through another year like 2005. Please not another year!"

It is an absolute miracle that I was able to overcome anxiety. God's hand has been on me, and I had no idea! He heard my cry and answered. Today, I give Him all the praise and glory! Even when we think we don't know Him, He knows us and He cares about every tiny or gigantic problem we face. Just call on Him!

Call unto me, and I will answer thee, and show thee great and mighty things, which thou knowest not.
—Jeremiah 33:3 KJV

Mental illness runs in my family. Some of my siblings take medication or have been in long-term therapy for depression and anxiety. It is nothing but a miracle that I suffered from anxiety and did not take medication for healing. Years later, I understood the deeper power of healing and why it had to happen that way! Besides my close friends, mother, and siblings, no one knew. Since that day, January 1, 2006, I was healed from full-blown anxiety attacks! I had about four mild episodes of anxiety early that year, but I ignored the sensation that I felt until the symptoms diminished completely, never to return again.

By the end of the year 2006, I started to become a bit more social. I started to go out more again and stopped being so serious all the time. I started hanging out with a younger guy who worked in the supermarket where I shopped every week. He was carefree, humorous, and mysteriously quiet at the same time, so it was nice being around him. My experiences with him reminded me of the childhood fun I never really experienced growing up, and boy, did I try to make up for that. We would take road trips to and travel out of state. We didn't talk about politics, education, or anything serious. We would just meet up and laugh all day about foolishness!

By September 2006, I was pregnant. I wanted to have a daughter and prayed for her. I envisioned my daughter and me wearing matching outfits. When I found out at four months that I was going to have a girl, I was ecstatic. Having my daughter and being engaged to be married a year later was exciting!

CHAPTER 4

Success: Whose Standards

ON JUNE 1, 2007, I graduated with a second master's degree. I did not attend the ceremony or any of my graduations since elementary school. I always thought it was the paper that mattered, not the event! Looking back, I realized that mindset was derived from not being celebrated, and so I learned to not celebrate myself. After graduating with a master's in library sciences, I took the state exam and became a certified school librarian.

The due date for the baby was June 11, but my baby was overdue and I ended up giving birth via caesarean section on June 28. That day was crazy because they called me in early to induce my labor since my water was low and Tracy was way overdue. The midwife said, "Let me just double-check your chart information one more time before we begin the induction." Then she said quickly, "Whoa, whoa! We will not be inducing your labor. You have to have a caesarean. Why didn't you tell me that you had a myomectomy the year before!"

I wanted to say, "That information is in my chart. Why didn't the doctor inform you!" But I was grateful that she caught that in the nick of time. Anyway, later that evening, I gave birth to a beautiful 7-and-a-half pounds, 20 inches baby girl! Jeez! She was so fair-skinned, I was shocked. As months passed, she got some melanin, some color! Not that anything is wrong with white skin; it's just that I didn't imagine a baby so pale would come from my womb.

Things seemed great. We were planning a wedding. First, we were going to have a small wedding in New York. Then the fights increased, so the engagement was off only to be back on. Then we planned a destination wedding. Money from friends was collected and down payments were made to have a small destination wedding in Jamaica.

But on Christmas Eve, he changed his mind, so the wedding was canceled. That was very hurtful, and I know that the relationship took a turn, and things were never quite the same.

We got back together again. I recall being totally unsure about going through with the wedding. My friend would say, "Theresa, normally, I wouldn't tell anyone what to do when it comes to marriage, but don't do it!" She was concerned because, as an unofficial wedding planner, she observed my lack of interest in picking out my dress and my dragging of my feet to send out the invitations, which were red flags to her.

Nevertheless, we got back together and got married in New York when Tracy was one years old. We argued before the wedding and even at the reception. I remember the maître d' asking me who picked out the song. He was taken aback by the Stevie Wonder "Ribbon in the Sky" song because he thought we were young and that song was before our time. The song didn't match the couple we were! Because we missed the regular cocktail hour, the wedding party, which consisted of a few of us, had to eat in a separate area upstairs where they sent up the food. I will never forget the maître d's statement. He said, "I don't know. I don't know, how you guys are going to make it!" You see, he saw the disconnection. He saw for certain that we were not on one accord. He boldly, without any reservation, said, "I have seen many weddings, and I'm telling you, this one is something!"

I was not offended. I could have complained, and his job could probably have been in jeopardy because his comments were inappropriate. But when you're faced with the ugly truth and he was speaking what I sensed to be true, why bother to fight? My significant other was somewhere with his friends, enjoying the flow of drinks. At some point, the maître d' was frustrated, looking all over for him so we could cut the cake together. It was a complete mess. I was miserable! Our marriage was always shaky. No one person is to blame. We were not equally yoked. I didn't know the biblical concept of the term, "equally yoked," but I knew in my heart that the back and forth of breaking up and getting back together and the constant disagreements were simply due to incompatibility, which led to an unstable marriage. I wanted to walk away but the pressure was also at play. I foolishly wanted to impress the world by showing everyone that although we had a child before wedlock, we are redeemed because we got married.

On the day of the wedding, God was talking. After everyone left the house, suddenly, our street got blocked, so the limousine couldn't drive up my street to pick up my bridal party and me. Of all the weekends to get married, we unknowingly chose Old Timers' Day in which, every year, the last weekend in July, at around 2:00 p.m., the streets around my area are blocked off. Everyone was waiting at the church for me to arrive, but I was stuck in the house for two hours, waiting for the limo. The limo never came because the blocked streets prevented it from coming across Linden Boulevard. Thank God the photographer was still at the house with me and had an SUV. He drove us in the opposite direction of our one-way street just to get us on the main street, Linden Boulevard. When we got there the police tells him, "You can't enter because all the streets are blocked. No cars can drive along here!"

I started yelling and waving my bouquet of flowers, "I'm two hours late for my wedding. Can't you allow us to drive just a few blocks?" It was actually about a mile down Linden Boulevard to Kings Highway where we needed to go.

The kind police officer said to my photographer, who suddenly became our chauffeur, "Okay. Since it's your wedding, drive behind me. I'm going to escort you to Kings Highway. I'm going to drive through all the lights. Just keep following me and drive."

I exhaled and was scared because we were driving at least 80 mph, breaking all the lights whether red, yellow, or green, but the streets were barricaded, so we felt a little safe. It was like a scene from a movie. When I arrived at the church, everyone looked upset because it was a very hot July day, and they waited in the hot sanctuary that was not air-conditioned for way too long.

After the ceremony, the limousine finally arrived, but then, no one was able to drive the usual route to Queens where the reception was being held. Apparently, there was an Amber alert that blocked off parts of the highway, causing heavy traffic congestion. We had to drive from Brooklyn through Far Rockaway to get back over to Queens Village.

We arrived very late and missed cocktail hour, but the maître d' set aside some food for us, the wedding party, because we were hungry. God was speaking, but I did not know His voice yet! That day was disastrous as if the wedding was not supposed to have taken place!

A few days after the wedding, the pastor called to tell us that we forgot to sign the certificate at the end of the ceremony, so our wedding is not really official! Ironic enough, less than a year after he married us, the church terminated him because they found out he was just a theology professor and not an ordained clergy, called to pastor.

After the wedding, we were trying to make our way to Las Vegas for our honeymoon. We missed our flight because I thought we had an evening flight, but in actuality, we had an earlier flight. We were on stand-by. I remember the airline had one seat left on the next plane to Las Vegas. They wanted to send one of us ahead, and the other would catch the next stand-by flight. I thought and said to the airline representative, "There is no way we are separating to start our honeymoon. We'll wait until there are two seats available for us on the same flight because we ain't splitting up!"

We waited for hours and hours. After the frustration of waiting, we checked in at a nearby hotel by the airport and waited for another four hours. We got so frustrated that we ended up canceling our trip to Las Vegas and drove to Atlantic City for our honeymoon!

The Bible tells us that what God has joined together, let no man separate. My deeper lesson is to know God's voice. When making life-changing decisions, know for sure that God ordained them. Were my connection and marriage joined by God or was it my own selfish desire? That's a rhetorical question that makes me evaluate all my relationships.

I was wrong for trying to project righteousness over what is right, and it cost us deeply. The emotional and financial pain was almost irreparable.

After a year of marriage, we separated for six months and then got back together. We managed because we had goals and plans. He was back in school, pursuing his bachelor's degree. I was saving, so we could buy a house in Connecticut. We traveled, and he visited Jamaica for the first time. Things were going well. I was pregnant again but had a miscarriage. Three years passed, and we were ready to buy a house, not in Connecticut but in Queens. We signed a contract to purchase the house in May, and I got pregnant in June. We bought the house in August 2012 when I was about three months pregnant. Having a house, a baby on the way, and financial responsibilities that increased by 200 percent suddenly not only tested the strength of our marriage but tested my faith.

What happened after that changed my life and flipped the core of who I thought I was completely. I am a different person today from the young, insecure girl, the one molested by a building super, the one often neglected because it appeared I didn't need anything, and the one who suffered and overcame anxiety. I am different because of the shaking that took place.

It seemed like I was successful according to the world's standards because we achieved the American dream of obtaining a house and having a healthy beautiful daughter and a son on the way. I had the degrees, a stable career, and a husband. As an African American immigrant, these accomplishments are what many aspire to achieve. We appeared to be a young, successful couple as others often complimented us and showed their admiration. But deep down inside, I was yearning for something deeper that none of the material things I have acquired fulfilled.

When I was in my early twenties, I would read about faith. I would read a lot of Iyanla Vanzant books. I was captivated by the New Age movement. It was so much a part of my life that when Iyanla Vanzant visited and spoke in New York, I was there. I purchased all her books, and of course, she autographed many of them. Her books are great teaching tools and helped me to grasp the concept of faith, but I felt the need to search for some more.

Back in 1995, I was dating a gentleman who was a member of The Nation of Islam. He dropped his "slave name" and had already legally changed his government name to a Muslim name. He had a lot of influence on me and tried to get me to change my name and follow his way of life. I was so close to changing my name, but he was so harsh with me that I got turned off by the idea. I was no longer allowed to wear short skirts or pum pum shorts. I had to wear long skirts to my ankles at all times. He didn't want me to appear happy in public. I remember him telling me after we returned from the movies, "Stop smiling in public. The black man has no reason to smile. Smiling is the white man's way of keeping us confused to be happy about our pathetic state."

He was ignorant and so controlling that I not only changed my mind about the name change but broke up with him. I disagreed and rejected his religious ideologies. May I say this because I didn't believe then, nor do I believe now, that all Muslims think the way he did, but I knew that his practice of faith was not for me.

I was searching but didn't want anything to do with any religion, specifically Christianity, which didn't make sense because my closest friends were mostly Christians. I was drawn to their humble spirit and sincerity but didn't want to fellowship as they did. Or was it I was rebellious and didn't want to surrender to God's will over my own? Once in a while, they would invite me to their church or a Bible study. I would always say, "No. I believe in God but not religion." I would even try to debate with some of my friends about their doctrine, which I referred to as "a book of fables." Yet they never judged or coerced me into believing what they believed. My stubbornness and ignorance did not stop them from loving me. They just continued to demonstrate pure, genuine, and sincere love. Throughout my process, they are still my closest friends after all these years.

I started reading a lot about Buddhism and intentionally applied the dharma practices to my life, which emphasize being kind and compassionate. Then I foolishly would go overboard with kindness, which led to many times being taken advantage of! I needed the wisdom to find balance. I continued to read over and over again *The Seven Spiritual Laws of Success* by Deepak Chopra, another influential spiritual leader, and found that he was saying basically the same things Iyanla Vanzant was saying! It was then that I was able to articulate the conclusion that was revealed to me that material things did not fulfill my soul.

The world tells us that success is about having material things in abundance, specifically, a lot of money, great jobs, popularity, and great relationships. Nothing is wrong with desiring the above things. However, if one has acquired those things for self-gratification and still feels empty, are you really successful? What will it take to be and feel fulfilled? After acquiring some things from my "Things to Accomplish" list, I have concluded that my definition of success does not line up with the world's definition of success. What is the point of having things and status but still feeling empty? What is the point of having things and still feeling like something is missing, only to get more things and still feeling empty?

Success is peace in the midst of trouble, joy despite the pain, and the ability to love regardless of whatever good or bad circumstance you're facing. This type of success yields contentment that does not come from the world; it comes from within.

God heard my calling for Him when I was five years old in Jamaica, when I returned from a holiday convention with a stretched-out hand to the sky, asking, "Who are you, but who are you?" He heard my calling to Him when I diligently sought him even in the wrong places, like in religion and relationships. But He answered my cry to him when I cried out during the most difficult trial of my life. It had to happen that way because I have been stubborn and rebellious. He was there all along, but I wanted to follow my own path. God had to trouble the waters, ruffle the feathers, and turn my life upside down to get my attention, so I would surrender and answer the call. It was painful, but it had to happen that way. And I'm glad it did! This is the testimony of the events leading up to the calling of God in my life and my surrendering to His will.

CHAPTER 5

Working for My Good

EVERYTHING WAS GOING well. Friday afternoon was my last examination before my scheduled C-section. The examination showed that the baby's head was in position and I was healthy and ready to have the cesarean in a few days. The next day, Saturday morning, I started having cramps but wasn't sure because I never went through labor pain with my daughter, so I was not quite sure if I was in labor. After I realized I was contracting every eight minutes or so, I called my doctor and made my way to the hospital.

We arrived at about 10:00 a.m. One of the doctors examined me, determined that I was not dilating, and wanted to send me home. I was in such pain that I told my husband, "I'll go to the lobby and wait for our doctor, but I'm not going home." I insisted that I was in labor and my doctor was on his way to conduct the caesarean section. After my refusal to leave, the anesthesiologist came over and started questioning me in preparation for my obstetrician. Then I excused myself and went to the bathroom. While in the bathroom, I heard the anesthesiologist yelling at the doctor that wanted to send me home, "That woman is in labor. She can barely talk! Prep her for surgery now! We can't wait for her doctor!" He was an angel sent.

When I came out of the bathroom, they had the stretcher ready. Another head obstetrician came in, took over, and they began the preparation. Another anesthesiologist came to take over and administered the medicine. While I was in the operating room, not sure who was going to perform the surgery, my doctor finally showed up.

I was numbed but not asleep, so I heard some conversations. Upon my son's delivery, he cried for one second but then we didn't hear anything afterward. They said to me, "Congratulations. You have a son," then quickly ushered my husband out of the operating room.

I saw a glance of my son looking purplish gray when they handed him over to another doctor. She began running with him. I did not get to hold him or look him in his eyes! Then I heard my doctor saying to the anesthesiologists, "Don't express. Don't express!" They transferred me to the delivery and recovery room where I was just waiting to hear something.

My doctor was sitting directly in front of us, biting his nails. We kept asking him what was going on, but he said, "Something happened, but the pediatrician will come and explain." He did not look us in the eyes when talking to us, so we knew something was significantly wrong.

After fifteen minutes, the pediatrician explained that my baby swallowed something, and they had to transport him to another hospital because there is nothing they could have done there. I said to her, "What do you mean there is nothing you can do to help him here? This is Methodist hospital, one of the best hospitals in Brooklyn."

Then the pediatrician explained in such a calm tone that, in ten minutes, they will let us know whether my baby will be taken to Cornell Medical Center or New York-Presbyterian Hospital. They were not sure as of yet. Weeks later, I learned that where my son was going to be transferred to depended on the severity of possible brain damage.

In fifteen minutes, the pediatrician returned and explained that my son was going to New York-Presbyterian/Columbia University Medical Center in an ambulance with a resident doctor, a nurse, and, of course, the paramedic. They assured me that he was in good hands and that a nurse and resident, in addition to the paramedic, will take good care of him. They left Methodist hospital from Park Slope, Brooklyn, and arrived at NY-Presbyterian/Cornell Medical Center in Washington Heights in about twenty-five minutes.

That's unbelievably crazy fast! I thought. They must have broken every single light to arrive there so quickly. Since then, before the coronavirus pandemic, I have had a great level of respect and admiration for essential workers, specifically EMTs and paramedics who are not acknowledged and celebrated enough!

What they did not inform me and what I learned weeks after was that he went into cardiac arrest at birth and again on his way to the hospital. He had to be resuscitated in the ambulance because the breathing machine that he was on jammed. I didn't even know that there was also a cord prolapse involved. So much was going on at his birth.

The doctors at NY-Presbyterian/Cornell Medical Center called me to get my verbal consent to conduct a number of life-saving procedures. First, they informed me that my son Terrence's oxygen level was dropping, and he was not getting the oxygen on the conventional ventilator so they need to place him on an ECMO. They also needed my verbal consent to conduct brain cooling because he lost so much oxygen. The brain cooling procedure would at least slow down the effect of possible brain damage. My response, in a very nasty attitude, was, "Yes yes. Do whatever you need to do. I give my consent in advance to whatever procedures you need to do!"

They explained the risk of a brain hemorrhage. They also said they would call me back in about two hours to inform me if he was able to sustain the ECMO.

After I got off the phone, I called my aunt Ivy. It is good, not just good but necessary to have someone in your life who you can call on any time of the day to pray for you. My aunt always prayed extensively during our Thanksgiving dinner, and we would secretly make faces because she took too long praying when we were hungry. She is the aunt that gave my siblings and me Bibles one year for our Christmas gifts. She was the one that came to my mind when I needed someone to intercede with! She was always a very busy woman and hard to catch, so thank God she answered her phone. I explained to her the situation, and she began to pray.

We were on the phone for about twenty minutes. She prayed so much that I was in and out of sleep. All I kept hearing her say was "In Jesus's name. In Jesus's name." Just before hanging up, she said, "Your son is going to live and will be home soon." She said, "Don't worry. He'll be home in a week."

I hung up the phone and cried out, "JESUS! JESUS! They say you do miracles. If you save my son and let him live a normal life, I promise I will go to church!"

I don't know where going to church came from or why I uttered those words. Maybe it was because I heard my aunt praying and calling Jesus's name. All I know is that I always thought of Jesus as a mythical character. I thought the Bible was a book of fables, and that many roads lead to God, not one. My thinking about faith and God did not include Jesus, but yet when I was in my most desperate state, I called on him.

After four hours of waiting to hear whether my son lives or dies, I called the hospital. The doctor said, "Not calling you is a good sign. You don't want us to call you right now. It wouldn't be good. We're doing all we can. We will call you as soon as there is some stability."

The entire night went by, and it was Sunday morning around 10:00 a.m. I haven't heard from the doctors in almost twelve hours, which gave me a little hope. That little hope turned into great faith like never before. All those years, I read about faith and tried to study it, but now it was time to exercise faith. This was the beginning of my walk of faith, a bumpy road on an unplanned journey.

By Monday, I was released from the hospital in Brooklyn and made my way straight uptown. When we arrived at New York-Presbyterian/Cornell Medical Center, we had no idea how dire my son's situation was until we got off the elevator and entered the NICU (neonatal intensive care unit).

Upon walking in, the nurses asked who we were, and I told them. They looked at us in disbelief as if they were staring at aliens. She started to inform the doctors that Baby Tulloch's family is there. We were looking around at all the babies that were mostly premature and very small. Over, in the far corner, away from the other premature babies was a baby placed on something like a cart. He was not in a regular crib. About five people, all dressed in black suits with clipboards in their hands, were surrounding this baby. Only one doctor was dressed differently but still not in the appropriate doctor's uniform. She approached my husband and me as the chief doctor or doctor in charge and began to explain.

"There is your son," referring to the baby the strangers in black suits were standing over. She began to explain, "They are all doctors. Some flew in to see what's going on."

It was like something from a movie. The chief doctor began to speak and explained tremblingly and nervously and very slowly, "Terrence was very, very sick when he came in. He was what we consider clinically deceased. He is on the ECMO. ECMO is short for extracorporeal membrane oxygenation and is used to function as his lungs and heart." She continued, "We had to stop his heart and drain his blood because his lungs are filled with meconium (feces when in the womb)." Then she said, "We normally keep babies on the ECMO for seventy-two hours."

I was looking at her like it was almost seventy-two hours. Then I asked, "What happens if he doesn't improve after seventy-two hours?"

She barely responded but said, "We'll see what happens then." She assured us that Terrence was under twenty-four-hour observation by a nurse that is only assigned to him and two resident doctors, whom we met.

The machine was situated between the two residents which enabled them to observe every movement of the machine in case of any slight changes while the machine went to work draining out his contaminated blood. It looked like two tubes were inserted into his neck artery. I was able to see the mud-colored blood pass out of his body through the tube, for what appeared to be filtering in the machine then back through the other tube showing the clean blood from the machine infused back into his body. I called it blood cleansing, but that was the least of his issue. At birth, he weighed 6 ½ pounds but by Monday three days after his birth, he was down to about 3 pounds.

I did not know nor could have known it at the time because I did not have the spiritual gift of wisdom, discernment, or understanding. yet. My son's life-saving process in the natural was parallel to my life-saving process in the spirit realm. God was doing work in both of us at the same time so that we could live to live again!

While my son was being healed physically through the draining of the contaminated blood in his body, God was cleansing me spiritually by applying the spiritual blood of Jesus over my life.

While on the ECMO, Terrence was also undergoing brain cooling. Brain cooling is a process of freezing the brain or wrapping a cooling cap around the baby's head to avoid brain damage due to the loss of oxygen. God was up to something, and I felt it. The doctors felt they wanted to take a chance and leave him on the ECMO for a little longer than seventy-two hours.

Terrence was on the ECMO for six days. On the seventh day, the doctors were thrilled to take him off the ECMO and place him on the oscillating respirator. There was hope! Terrence improved and then was able to get on the ventilator.

After a few weeks, Terrence was improving in the area of breathing in oxygen, but he had issues breathing out carbon dioxide, so he was on the CPAP (continuous positive airway pressure) for an extensive period of time. The doctors couldn't figure out what was causing him to not progress and come off the CPAP. There were some concerns on the table that included heart disease, chronic lung disease, brain damage, and neurological issues, but the prayer had already gone up, the Word went out, and God had already answered despite the seesaw progress we saw!

Terrence overcame what was thought to be brain damage and chronic lung disease due to meconium aspiration. There was a serious concern about heart issues, but the test results showed he overcame that too.

Many years before, my cousin had given my mother a small little book that lists multiple scriptures about healing. The book is titled, *God's Creative Power for Healing*, by Charles Capps. My mother told me to read the book and to continue reading it every day. I was just saved, four days earlier when I called "Jesus, Jesus, if you save my son, I will go to church!" I was not familiar with scripture, but something told me (later understood it was the Holy Spirit for sure) to copy the page with the scripture and tape it onto his crib (wasn't even a typical baby crib) while he was on the ECMO.

When God saves us, He begins to direct our path in a way that we are able to hear His voice and take actions that are aligned with His will for our lives.

I began to read out loud the scripture over my son every single day. I didn't really understand them at first; but felt, deep down inside, it was necessary for his healing. Soon after, I was quoting scripture, such as, "We overcome by the blood of the lamb and the word of our testimony." So when Terrence was on the roller-coaster ride of getting better one day only to regress the next day. The Word gave me the faith to believe that supernatural healing had already taken place, especially since he had come from so far. "Clinically deceased," the doctor had said.

I remember one nurse saying, "When Terrence was brought in, I worked harder than any other day in my nursing career. He kept me on my feet all night, but we are not out of the woods." Her comments that we are not out of the woods did not frighten me because I kept on reading God's word. I read it and believed it. My faith was activated. It was like a light switch was suddenly turned on.

Here are some other scripture taken from *God's Creative Power to Heal* by Charles Capps that was read over Terrence during the two months he was in the hospital. I would read aloud the Word and insert Terrence's name in place of the pronoun "my" to ensure that I was praying specifically for Terrence.

"Jesus took my infirmities and bore my (Terrence's) sicknesses. Therefore, I refuse to allow sickness to dominate my (Terrence's) body. The Life of God flows within me (Terrence) bringing healing to every fiber of my (Terrence's) being" (Matt. 8:17 and John 6:63).

I would read every day, "I am but instead say (Terrence is) redeemed from the curse. Galatians 3:13 is flowing in my (Terrence's) bloodstream. It flows to every cell of my (Terrence's) body, restoring life and health."

The above word was written on page 26 of Charles Capps's book, taken from the Bible (Mark 11:23 and Luke 17:6).

My faith was getting so strong that, although my son did not come home after a week as my aunt thought, it didn't matter to me. I believed he was coming home completely healed, and time was not an issue.

Every Saturday, a different family member would come with me to visit. After visiting him, we would go across the street to the same wonderful pizza shop and eat, drink, and be merry. They asked, "How could you celebrate and at the same time deal with this nightmare?" During the ups and downs of his healing, my friend Gloria always said, "You don't understand this, but all of this is going to work out for your good and for God's glory."

Faith without works is dead, the Bible says. I learned quickly that If I'm going to profess faith, my faith will be tested.

My son was having difficulty getting off CPAP, and it didn't make any sense. One of his nurses recognized that his cry made a weird hoarse sound. Upon examination, they saw that the opening part of his trachea was oval in shape instead of round, which was attributed to his needing to stay on the CPAP. The care was not the same at the hospital because he was no longer in a life-threatening situation as when he arrived. When they took him off of the CPAP, his oxygen level would drop.

One of the nurses, a Godsent, pulled me to the side and said, "His state is not as critical, so maybe you should consider transferring him back to his birth hospital. He will heal completely, but he needs the time and special attention to be weaned off."

I was not sure what to do because NewYork-Presbyterian/Cornell Medical Center at Stanley Morgan is rated one of the top children's hospitals in the country, the world rather. Why would I transfer him from the best of the bests? Sometimes practicing faith will appear illogical. I prayed on it and took that leap of faith to have him transferred back to Brooklyn where he was born. After all this time, which was about seven weeks later, the same exact paramedic who brought Terrence uptown in the ambulance where the breathing machine had jammed on the way was the same paramedic who was taking him back to Methodist hospital where he was born. What was astounding was that the paramedic recognized Terrence and was so thrilled. He joked, "At least, he's not going back with doctors and nurses the way he left!"

They arrived at 4:00 p.m., and I met up with them at around 6:00 p.m. At the midnight hour, I received a call from one of the nurses. She said, "We have great news! We took Terrence off the CPAP just to see how he would do, and his oxygen level has been stable at 97 percent." He never got back on the CPAP and was released to go home a few days later. They sent him home on .01 percent oxygen, just in case, but Terrence kept snatching out the nasal cannula from his nose because God answered the prayer. He was fully and completely healed and didn't need it. To God be all the glory!

CHAPTER 6

Really, Really

WE HAVE BEEN home with our son for two months and decided to present him to the Lord as soon as possible. We wanted him christened right away, like yesterday. We asked one pastor of the church that my husband visited to christen him. He wouldn't give us an answer right away. He kept telling us, "Come to Bible study, and I will let you know my answer."

We were going to service and Bible study for two weeks straight and kept asking, but he still insisted that we continue to attend Bible study before we get an answer.

After waiting for three weeks and too much frustration, I began asking around. My sister Kimone was saved and already had a church she attended every week, so I started complaining to her. After complaining to her, she stepped in right away and said, "Don't worry. I'm going to ask my pastor to christen him, and I know he's going to say yes. Trust me. He's not going to have you waiting!"

She called him right there and then. I was shocked that she had the pastor's number in her phone but more impressed that he picked up the phone and his response was, "Let me check my calendar and give you the exact date. I know it's going to be the second Sunday of the month!"

Then I was shouting over the phone, "Ask him how much money it's going to cost!"

He heard and told Kimone, laughing, "Tell your sister we don't charge to do baby dedications!"

Just like that Terrence was Christened two weeks later on July 14, 2013.

I was taken aback because everything inside the church looked old and tattered, but there was a sense of holiness. A bunch of women were dressed in all white. I remember the pastor lifting Terrence up, praying for him. He thanked God for allowing Terrence to be healed and thanked God that his name was taken off the church's prayer list.

I said to myself, "One day, I'm going to come back here!"

The entire summer passed, and I did not step foot in that church or any other church. Every Sunday, I kept saying to myself, "I know we need to go and bring the kids." I felt the pull to go but just didn't feel like going.

Summer passed, and I went back to work in September. On the second week of back to school, I got sick. Actually, there was a tiny little bump on my toe. For no reason, I took a pin and popped it, not knowing that the pin was contaminated. The next day, I was in pain and couldn't go to work. The following day, it got severe. By day three, I was in excruciating pain and couldn't walk properly. Let me say this, I have had two caesareans and a hysterectomy in which an incision was made in the same area three different times, causing great pain and still I have never felt pain like the one from my infected toe. The infection was traveling and the pain was unbearable.

I went to one doctor's office, and they couldn't help me so they advised me to seek a podiatrist. My foot was swollen, and I wasn't able to walk without crutches. The podiatrist prescribed antibiotics but after three days, my foot became more swollen, and the antibiotics were not working. I ended up going to the emergency room.

They attempted to drain it and gave me an IV and another kind of antibiotic along with oxycodone, the super painkiller. All along, I would send the podiatrist pictures of my foot for her to evaluate the swelling and determine if the infection was clearing up.

It was a Thursday night and I was in unbearable pain. I couldn't even take care of the baby. Thank God my aunt was visiting from Florida, and she has been the caretaker. Every night, she would have us pray before going to sleep. After she prayed and left, I remembered Jesus and what he did for Terrence. I managed to get on my knees (it took awhile to maneuver to that position). I lifted up a simple and bold prayer, asking God, "Jesus, please, please, heal my foot. I promise if you heal me, I will start going to church."

The next morning, I took a picture and sent it to my podiatrist. She called me and started shouting enthusiastically, "The medicine is working. Your foot is healing. You're getting better!"

I asked her, "How do you know I'm healing because I'm still in a lot of pain and my foot is still so swollen?"

She explained that she was able to notice lines despite the swelling. My foot was like a balloon, but the lines, which were not there the day before, were an indication that the swelling was subsiding. Dr. Dee attributed the healing to the medicine, which indeed was the catalyst, but I knew it was God's healing power at work again. That was Friday morning, and three days later, on Sunday, I made my way to church on crutches and never looked back.

I'm a church girl now. Wow! Who would have thought! I started attending service regularly at the end of September and officially joined in November, the week before Thanksgiving. By December, I was working on assignments with the children there, not knowing that this would have been my Egypt experience.

There was praise that had to be released out of my mouth. It was on the tip of my tongue, and when I entered the sanctuary, His presence was there. I didn't care who saw or heard me. At first, I tried to be dignified and sit quietly. After about two services, I couldn't contain myself. I would stand during worship, lift up my hands, and shouts of "Hallelujah" were made! I found myself dancing in the aisle, something that they didn't do there.

Every Sunday, I had to be there and thought, How on Earth did I miss all of this my whole life? It was wonderful; it was the presence of God!

The church had children, including my niece and daughter, who attended every week, but they did not provide Sunday school. Soon I was their Sunday school teacher. Suddenly, I was asked to serve as a deaconess. What should have been a blessing ended up being a test of faith that almost led me astray from serving in the church.

Suddenly, I found myself behind the scenes, exposed to all sorts of things not worthy to be mentioned. There was division, dissension, jealousy, and hatred among the brethren. It was shocking and contradictory to my preconceived idea of Christian culture. It took years for me to understand that what happens outside of the church also happens inside the church. It took years for me to understand that the church is a place where people come in broken (like myself) with levels of issues needing to be healed and made whole. It took years for me to really understand that through the working of the Holy spirit, and if we allow the Holy spirit to truly operate, the church is where transformation should take time.

I wanted to gracefully walk away from the deaconess in training position but was reminded that "People have been waiting for over twenty-five years to be where you are, and you're thinking about passing it up? Are you crazy!" They looked at the position the way one would look at a promotional position in a corporation.

It was a place of worship but heavily rooted in tradition. Every week, the pastor would preach a great word, but did the word penetrate the hearts of everyone? I just got saved and was trying to serve God while clinging to my broken marriage.

I needed healing and deliverance and had no patience for the endless arguments about things that had nothing to do with God. For example, arguing about which combination of colors to wear for Women's Day or arguing about who should get leftovers and who should not! I didn't have the maturity or wisdom to go into prayer and intercede right there and then. Behind the scene was crazy! I told the pastor I didn't know how I was going to continue. He would try to encourage me and say, "You and your sister are agents of change. That's all!"

My sister Kimone had walked in "from off the street," as they would say, and joined the church about a week after he became the pastor. He would say, "You and your sister are from a different cloth, and that's what it takes to change some traditions."

Foolishly, and I say foolishly because I did not have the spiritual maturity nor the authority to handle the change that I thought needed to take place. Nevertheless, I would subtly ask, "Is that what the Bible says or hints to that effect?"

They started looking at me sideways, the way they looked at the individuals they warned me about. I was like, "Really, really. So now you're gonna treat me the same way you treat your so-called enemies around here?" It was a battle to serve and at the same fellowship.

I left that church prematurely. God did not release me, but I left out of frustration and disappointment. I was without a church home for six months. I visited dozens of churches throughout New York City, but couldn't find a place to settle. I developed a prayerful life, praying daily, and started talking to God the way I talk to a friend, a confidant. Just before New Year's Eve, I heard the Lord say, "Go back and be still!"

In retrospect, I remember the vow I made to the Lord: "If you save my son, I will go to church!" God answered my prayer because it was His will to reveal himself to me through that circumstance. That was His way of getting my total and undivided attention.

Know therefore that the Lord thy God, He is God, the faithful God, which keepeth covenant and mercy with them that love Him and keep His commandments to a thousand generations.
—Deuteronomy 7:9 KJV

God is a covenant keeper and faithful to His promises. God was so faithful to me during my darkest hour; there was no way I intended to break my vow to him. The enemy tried with all his might to keep me out of the church but he did not prevail.

While I thought they were the problem, God used the circumstance to teach me lifelong lessons about humility, love, patience, and obedience!

On New Year's Eve 2016, my sister and I went back. The pastor was happily surprised, and our sisters and brothers, who we love much, were very receptive. Some came off the choir stand to hug us. Some were crying and told us they missed us and that we shouldn't let anyone steer us away. I missed them as well.

I returned to my home church a little more mature in God after visiting so many churches. Most importantly, I returned filled with the Holy Ghost but wasn't aware of the power that was in me. God never shows us everything at once. He doesn't show us the end of a thing; instead, he unveils us little by little as we journey through life.

> **I make known the end from the beginning, from ancient times, what is still to come. I say, "My purpose will stand, and I will do all that I please"**
> —Isaiah 46:10 NIV

It all happened in the summer of 2015. I was visiting my aunt, Ms. Senior in Florida. She is the same aunt whose house we frequently visited in Long Island when we were young. She is the same aunt who, when Terrence was in the hospital after a month, had me recite the salvation prayer over the phone to ensure my salvation.

Tracy, Terrence, and I visited her on vacation and went to a Tuesday or Wednesday evening service at her church, Maranatha Christian Center, Melbourne, Florida. After service, my aunt introduced me to her pastor and said to him, "This is my nephew, the baby you all were praying for on the prayer list." Then her pastor prayed for Tracy and Terrence again. Afterward, one of the leaders asked if I wanted to come up for prayer too and my aunt asked me if I wanted to receive the Holy Spirit.

Yikes! Petrified is an understatement of how I felt at that moment. I didn't know what that meant, to receive the Holy Spirit, but I was nervous.

They began to pray and speak in tongues. I was crying, and after a long while, I started making some *sss* sounds. It took awhile, but they kept praying, and suddenly, I started speaking in what they call tongues. After they finished praying, the pastor said, "God bless you, Sister. You have just received the Holy Spirit!"

I had no idea of the significance of it. I was in the faith for almost two years and knew what a good sermon sounded like. I heard about people speaking in tongues, but I didn't know what it meant to receive the Holy Spirit and its power. I wasn't moved or had a response that showed great gratitude either. At the end of the service, the pastor gave me a small booklet titled, *God's Will Is the Holy Spirit* by Gloria Copeland and encouraged me to read it. On the car ride back home, my aunt explained what it meant. Unfortunately, I didn't read the little booklet until a year later.

Upon returning to my home church, I told the pastor I would like to just sit in the back pew and worship because God directed me to be still. He understood. A few weeks later, they, the same individuals who frustrated me to the point of leaving inquired about my being a trustee. My answer was simply no! I knew I was not sent back to serve as a trustee or deaconess or Sunday school teacher or in any other title position. The Lord directed me to come back home and be still. I interpreted it as not getting involved in the behind-the-scene things. Ultimately, I wanted God. I wanted a relationship with Him and certainly did not want anything to do with titles or positions.

My worship and praise were the same, but occasionally, the speaking of tongues would come out during praise. That same individual who came to church to provoke people as if we were in junior high school whispered one Sunday, "We don't speak in tongues here. It's demonic!"

In my mind, I was like, "Really, really. They're still doing this, still gossiping in the sanctuary, still making negative comments about people!" I wasn't weak anymore though, so I continued to worship and waited for the Lord, not knowing exactly what I was waiting for.

But they that wait upon the Lord shall renew their strength; they shall mount up with wings as eagles; they shall run and not be weary, and they shall walk and not faint.
—Isaiah 40:31 KJV

Although I made a decision to not do anything behind the scene, it was my pastor's fifth pastoral anniversary, and he asked me to write a poem for him and recite it during service. The poem was written with all intentions to honor my then-pastor, but as the words flowed, the message switched. The poem ended up being an expression of the change that needed to take place for our spiritual growth.

The Gift of Grace

Thank you, Father God
For blessing us

With a pastor
That preaches and teaches
Us
About Jesus
He leads us
From glory to glory
Where we feel more
Of your holiness
Oh yes, indeed
We are
Blessed
To be here
Celebrating this
5th Pastoral Anniversary
Especially since
The number five symbolizes
God's grace
This grace is evident
When God gave us
The first five books
Of the Bible
Also known as
The Pentateuch
But we as humans
Are weak in the flesh
We continue to fall
So God gave us
Another gift
The greatest gift
Of them all

This gift is Salvation
Through Jesus Christ
By faith
That's enough reason

To stand on our feet
Right now and
Celebrate
Salvation is a free
Gift
All one has to do
Is open his heart
Believe
Repent
And then
Receive Him
In addition
This is the year 2017
And the number seventeen
Symbolizes victory
Victory over
Seen and unseen
Enemies
So no matter what
Trials or tribulations
That we encounter
We are under Grace
Which means
We have the victory
In all situations
But in order to experience
The fullness of God's grace
We have to be careful
We're not caught up in
Tradition
Or religion
Or spiritual rituals
Or sometimes even
Positions
Positions that could

THERESA TULLOCH

Have us complacent
So much that we
Can't even trace Him
Him who is the Father,
The Son, and the Holy Spirit
So let us begin with
Redirecting
Our focus
On the purpose
Why we are really here
Which is
To worship Him
Under the leadership
Of Pastor ***** Anointing
We are here to worship
Him
Pray to God
And Praise Him
In this place
We seek His face
As we run this race
And thank Almighty God
For this gift of
Amazing Grace

After the above poem was recited, the guest preacher brought forth a Word. The service was different from any other anniversary service. For one, the usual preacher who would come every year to preach was sick and sent someone in her place. No one knew who this guest preacher was. She began to preach. The message was, "Get Up and Walk," which was taken from the Bible in the book of John 5:1–9 about the Healing at the Pool. There was something different about this service. There was a shift in the atmosphere. Many guest preachers have visited and brought forth a powerful Word, but what happened was miraculous. People started asking, "Who is she? Where did this one come from?"

The lady behind me asked, "How come we never saw her before?" Another worshipper whispered. Close to the end of the sermon, the preacher called those wanting prayer to the altar.

My sister Kimone and I with about ten other people rushed to the altar. The preacher began to pray, speak in tongues, and lay hands on us. People were crying; everyone was up on their feet. It was a lively service like never before. Out of the twelve of us who were at the altar, three of us fell back under the unction of the Holy Spirit that was moving in the sanctuary.

Someone behind me caught me, so I did not fall all the way down. My older brother in Christ was strategically in the right place at the right time and caught me. I got up, speaking in tongues fluently and flowing nonstop. It was like a surge of electricity running through me. My pastor looked at me in disbelief. Since that service, my worship and praise have never been the same.

Unfortunately, the same two individuals, who commented that we don't speak in tongues up in here since it's demonic, and also the same individuals who antagonized others with their gossiping and negativity, missed the service. They missed the poem, which was really about refocusing on God again. They missed the powerful message that instructed us to "get up and walk." They missed the greatest move of God that our church has ever witnessed since my joining in 2013. Unfortunately, they were across the street, busy setting up the food for the luncheon to follow.

They were more concerned about physical food than spiritual food that changes lives. But I got what I needed from God that Sunday and kept on moving.

A few months later, I felt that I was under attack again and started asking God to deliver me from the hurt that comes with it. One week in August, I was at the altar, praying for God to release me, but this time, release me to another place of worship so that I have cover and not wander from church to church like I did the year before.

Three days later, on a Tuesday, I got acquainted with my daughter's close friend's father. I knew a little bit about him because my children and his children attended the same public school and after-school daycare center. We crossed paths at our children's daycare barbeque event and exchanged numbers. After our first personal conversation, I learned he was recently divorced like me, and he just happened to be an assistant pastor. We started dating. Figuring God was closing a door to open a new one, I went to my pastor immediately and asked him for his blessing to release me. He prayed, we cried, and I will never forget the words he said, "You have been called to ministry. That's why we pushed you into the deaconess position right away. But I'm telling you, ministry is not easy." He wished me all the best, gave me his blessing, and I was on my way!

I spent almost two years at my new church. Surely, God sent me there for a particular reason. The relationship with my boyfriend did not last. After one and a half years, we broke up. It was my action that led to the inevitable breakup. Looking back at the root of our relationship, God was not pleased with us. The Bible says, "Not many of you should become teachers, my fellow believers, because you know that we who teach will be judged more strictly" (Jas. 3:1 NIV).

I believe because we were living in sin, and God called him to a higher standard of accountability (assistant pastor); the relationship was doomed. After we broke up, I remained there for another six months. I learned my lesson the first time around, which is not to leave without a proper release (peacefully) or leave without a place to worship, for I need to be covered.

The power of God was prevalent though. There was much deliverance but I can't say much healing for me. Almost everyone spoke in tongues, including me, so I thought it was a good fit there. Every week, the pastor laid hands, and indeed, we would fall down under the unction of the Holy Spirit. There was no mimicking of falling. Sometimes, the pastor did not even have to lay hands, just standing in front of him was enough for us to fall. Upon falling, many of the younger sisters would vomit. I learned, according to my boyfriend, the assistant pastor, that throwing up was a sign of losing spirit (the ungodly spirit), which is a form of deliverance. Upon deliverance, sometimes the throat tightens and the sensation of wanting to throw up takes place, which is what causes the need to vomit. In that church, I experience a lot of falling, crying, screaming, and even crawling, but never any throwing up.

My experience at that place of worship was the extreme opposite of my first church. I always felt alone. Everyone in the church had an assignment except for me. The only task I had was to sometimes stand next to the younger sisters with a plastic bag because they were sure to vomit at the altar. It was a recurring experience every single week. Deliverance, then they would go out into the world and live their best life throughout the week, and then come back again on Saturday or Sunday for more deliverance, more vomiting.

I felt very isolated since the first day I stepped foot in that church. After the relationship ended, week after week, I would attend service and sit on the pew all by myself with no one to talk to. I felt scorned, like a woman with leprosy who is ostracized. After every service, I would run out the door to 7-Eleven to get coffee, but it wasn't the coffee that I really wanted. I needed to breathe fresh air. I felt stifled.

Those days were draining. My children and I were in service on Thursday nights from 7:30 to 9:00 p.m.; on Saturday nights, from 7:30 until God was finished with us; on Sunday mornings, from 11:00 a.m. to 2:00 p.m., and then again on Sunday nights, from 6:30 p.m. until God was finished with us.

My friends started to invite themselves one by one to visit because they were concerned and thought I was in a cult. I was not allowed to visit my sister in Maryland anymore, and it was frowned upon if I ever missed a service. I was very alone, very broken, and in need of emotional healing! It was after I left that place of worship that I realized the isolation was God's way to cocoon me first in preparation for the divine assignments that were about to be released. All along, He was breaking and making me into the woman He created me to be.

I started to look for the preacher who visited and preached for my former pastor's fifth anniversary. I couldn't remember her first name. All I knew was that her last name was Collins. I wanted to find her church because my days at my ex-boyfriend's place of worship had come to an end, but from past experience, I knew I had to wait for God to release me.

I spent months looking up Collins, using her name with various church terms in my search. Then I remembered that when she visited, she was introduced as overseer. Bingo! I found her, Overseer Collins. After months, I finally found her on YouTube. While I was cocooned and isolated at my second church, I was fed by the 3–10 minute video clips of her sermons that were posted on YouTube.

Finally, I found out where her church was and said to myself, "Oh well, I'm not going to the Bronx. That's too far. That's too much. I am not going there!" So I stayed at my place of worship spiritually dead! But God does not save us to be spiritually dead. He saves us so that we may have life and have life more abundantly.

One day, I was on a work assignment in which I was sent to score the state ELA and math tests that students in our district had taken. I was in the lobby of a neighboring school with about three hundred teachers from two school districts. I ran into a young lady who used to visit my first church. I knew she was a minister because she had visited and facilitated a women's day workshop for our church, which, in my opinion, was one of the best fellowship experiences we had in that church. She also recognized me, so we said hello to each other. Afterward, they divided about thirty teachers per classroom to begin scoring. I kept saying, "I don't feel like being friendly (I still struggle with anti-social issues), and I hope she doesn't end up in my room."

Of course, out of all the rooms on the two floors, this young lady ends up not only in my room but at the table across from me. I heard the Lord say, "Go and be friendly!" which is not easy for me to do! It's not my personality to approach people first and strike up a conversation (the spirit of rejection was still operating in me). I refused to go over to her table. I heard the Lord say, "Go over there and say hello!"

Although I did not want to go, when the Holy Spirit begins to frustrate you to do something outside of your comfort zone, you might as well surrender. So, reluctantly, I approached her table, and she said, "You're Theresa, right!" I responded and asked about her mother, who is also a member of my first church. Then I asked, "How is your ministry going?" She said everything was going well and invited me to attend a weekend retreat her ministry was hosting in Princeton, New Jersey. She handed me the flyer and told me I should try to attend. I looked at the flyer and almost fell out. I saw a picture and all the words, SPECIAL GUEST SPEAKER A—— Collins!

This is no coincidence! I thought to myself. I began to explain to the minister about how I was looking for this preacher for months, and I recently found her on YouTube, and have been watching her sermons. I told her, "I will make my way because I know this can't be a coincidence that I ran into you and you're giving me this flyer!" I knew God was up to something.

It was a two-day women's retreat, but I only attended the Saturday event. My friend, Theresa B., and I made our way to Princeton, New Jersey. There were a number of speakers teaching about mental health care and the importance of seeking professional help.

One particular speaker taught about getting to the root of our wounds. We were encouraged to trace the root of our wounds. We were also encouraged to allow our wounds to heal and not cover them with Band-Aids because covering doesn't mean we are healed, and we could be bleeding on others. In other words, if we are hurting and we don't check ourselves and get healed instead of covering the hurt, we might end up hurting others, especially those close to us. A number of presenters from the mental health field were there and reminded us that it is okay to seek therapy even for believers!

The last segment was allotted to the special guest speaker. Just like when she visited my first church for the pastor's fifth pastoral anniversary and tore up the place, she came in with the full power of God, anointed to heal and deliver. She touched every soul in the room. She preached and taught. She spoke about three types of women. Her message came from the Book of Ruth in the Bible. She spoke about Ruth, a woman who, despite her challenging circumstances, had great faith and wasn't afraid to move to the unknown. She spoke about Naomi, Ruth's mother-in-law, a woman who had everything but lost them and became so bitter that she changed her name to Mara, meaning God had left her. And she spoke about Orpah, Ruth's sister-in-law, a woman who, because of her challenging circumstances which were the same challenges as Naomi's and Ruth's, looked back and turned back to her old way of living, the life she had without the true, living God. As she spoke, I was like, "Oh my God! You are talking to me today Lord." I said to myself, "I'm in a spiritually dead situation, but I'm definitely not Naomi. I have hope always, and I'm not bitter. And I'm never going back to anything I was moved from so I know I'm not an Orpah. I think I'm a Ruth!"

I concluded that I was more like Ruth because I knew I had to move on from my current place of worship but was waiting for God to give me the revelation about when and where to go!

After her preaching on the three prototypes of women, she got into the prophetic. About all forty women in the room were lined up to hear a prophetic word. I was the fifth person. She said, "You are not at home where you are!"

I fell down before she finished speaking. The presence of God was so powerful in the room. I didn't remember what else was said. My friend Theresa B. said that she heard the part about not being at home. I knew what the prophecy meant though. The place where I was sitting on the pew by myself, completely ignored, with no task to do, intentionally left out, isolated, and rejected was not my church home. I was just passing through, and it was time to get up and move!

When God wants to do a thing in us, through us, and for us, despite our rebellious ways, He knows how to shake things up to get us to pivot in His direction and move according to His will!

My current place of worship at the time planned to have a Fourth of July barbeque at a local state park but did not invite me. The good thing about that was I was not offended! I looked at it as a door God was closing again because He wants to open a new one. I took some weeks off and, upon returning, told the pastor that I was moving on. He agreed that it was best. He said he knew that it was a matter of time and was expecting it. When I first joined his ministry, he prophesied that I was called to an elevated place. He once again reminded me about that prophecy, which confirmed what my first pastor had said when he released me. He said, "All I can say is you have been called to an elevated place!" That was his way of giving me his blessing, and I'm grateful for that. Those words gave me the strength to continue in ministry when sometimes I want to hang up the towel and run from it all.

The Bible tells us to trust God with all our hearts and lean not on our own understanding. In all our ways acknowledge him and he will lead our path (Prov. 3:5–6 KJV). I was reluctant to drive over the Whitestone Bridge, cross the East River, and go to the Bronx to worship, but I needed to be in the presence of the Lord, and I had to trust His way and direction.

I visited the Overseer's church the first week in August 2019, but she was not there. She was apparently on an assignment in Alabama, but the atmosphere was beautiful. In fact, we kept on circling the block six times, and I was ready to leave and go back home! Talk about running from the Lord! My daughter said, "Mommy why don't you turn right instead?" Sure enough, when I turned right, a parking spot was right there. After service, my daughter Tracy's response was, "Yes, this is it. This is where we're gonna be going!"

That was not the response I wanted to hear. I was hoping she wouldn't like it so that I would have a reason to run! But we can't run from God! No matter where we go, He is with us, so even if we try to run from Him, we only end up running into Him! He doesn't change His mind about us!

> **For the gifts and calling of God are without repentance.**
> **—Romans 11:29 KJV**

Perhaps you are reading this and wondering if you are called. Perhaps you already know that God called you and you're serving; but He is calling you to a higher place, the next level, but you are running. They say the first sign of your calling to God is running from it. We run from the calling of God because, at first, it might appear burdensome, or oftentimes, we feel unequipped to do whatever He wants us to do, which is often what we don't want to do or what we know we can't do with our own strength. God does not need our strength or our intellect. He wants our hearts. May I encourage you to trust God and say yes! Say yes and let God handle the details because He is going to have His way in your life anyway. We can't outsmart or outrun God. He is too big, too powerful, and ultimately, He created us for himself! If you are pondering about a calling with God in your life, may I encourage you to say this prayer:

> Father God, I come to you because
> I feel something stirring in my heart
> I sense that you are near
> Your Holy Word says, "Draw nigh to God
> And He will Draw Nigh to You"
> So here I am Lord Jesus
> I am an imperfect soul asking you to
> Forgive me for my sins
> Come into my heart and guide me
> Lead me in the way I should go
> Help me to walk into the calling
> You have on my life by the power of
> Your Holy Spirit
> I thank you, Lord, for
> Saving me and answering
> My prayer. Amen.

My sister Kimone, my two children, and I made our way to our second visit to Overseer's church in the Bronx. When we arrived, the doors were closed. I wanted to leave and go back home, but Kimone insisted that I call her.

At the end of the retreat, back in May, I met Overseer in person, introduced myself, and told her about my months of hearing her sermons online. We became Facebook friends, and sometimes, she would post a flyer about her speaking engagements. Because I had her phone number and we had spoken a few times via instant message, Kimone's response was, "Call her now because I didn't come all the way here just to turn around!"

"No, I'm not calling her because she's probably preaching somewhere, and I would be interrupting her," I said.

Kimone was like, "Give me your phone. I'm calling her!"

She called, and to our surprise, the church was having a Praise in the Park fellowship, which was why no one was at the church. She invited us to meet in the park. When we got there, the entire congregation was having a barbecue. Well, look at God again! The last straw for me at church number two was when they had a Fourth of July barbeque in a local state park and excluded me. Around seven weeks later, on August 24, 2019, I found myself in another local state park across the waters, attending church. It was at Pelham Bay Park, Bronx, New York. In the midst of the barbeque, the Overseer introduced us and announced to the entire congregation that we were new members of EPIC. It happened just like that!

I never told her the prophecies my previous pastors said about my calling. My intention was to just worship and go home; besides, if those prophecies are true, she would get the revelation as well because God is not the author of confusion! I was not ready to open up to church people so easily! Suddenly, Overseer had me conducting the opening prayer for service. The first time, I was nervous and stumbled on some words. The second time, I allowed the Holy Spirit to take over, and in the opening prayer, I kept saying "Yes, I surrender. Yes, I surrender," which was not really an opening prayer! Nevertheless, God had His way! I knew my days of timidity and my avoidance of speaking publicly was coming to an end.

After about one year, she started calling me Minister Theresa. She's given so many teachings on the power of a name and calls us as she sees us in the spirit. It is a great honor to be a minister (servant) of the Lord. I sensed the calling from the day I walked into my first church, but never fathom how on Earth it would come to pass. I was still very timid, still very insecure, and still struggling with social anxiety, so ministering to me was farfetched. But God revealed over time that ministering or serving is not always about speaking from the pulpit. I could minister through my poems and writing. We don't have to have it all together and be perfect to be used by God either. We just have to have a willing heart. In fact, when we serve God in our weakness, He gets all the glory because His strength is made perfect through our weakness. We are just vessels that He uses to get His will done, and to me, that is the greatest honor!

CHAPTER 7

No Means No!

IN SEPTEMBER 2021, I transferred to another library position at a combined middle and high school. My colleague, whose office is next to the library, serves as a social worker and invited me to listen to his podcast F.A.C.T.S., which is the acronym for "Factual, Authentic, Captivating, Transformative Stories." The episodes are relevant and provide various points of view on a range of topics—such as fashion trends, technology, emotional, social, financial, and even relationship issues, just to name a few. What makes the podcast unique is that the topics are sometimes serious and inspirational but, at the same time, delivered with a light and humorous touch. In one episode entitled "Testimony," the guest speaker decided to release his testimony about a time in his life he was accused of raping someone he was currently dating and how God brought him out of the trial, which was really a test of faith for him. Upon hearing the podcast, I had to respond to my colleague and let him know that I did not only believe his friend, the guest speaker, but I was on the opposite end of rape! That podcast opened the door for me to express what happened to me and release the emotional hurt that many victims, like myself, easily suppress.

When I got saved in 2013 and filled with the Holy Ghost in 2015, I did not change completely. Transformation is an inner work that the Lord does over time. I got divorced in 2014 before my son turned one years old. I was saved but, sometimes, still yearned for fleshly desires.

In 2016, my neighbor from down the block across the street started conversing briefly with a simple hello here and there and a "How are you" whenever I would be going in and out of my house. I didn't know at the time, but he told me he was always watching me and observed the day my ex-husband moved out the year before. That should have been a red flag! He would offer to help me with my car issues after witnessing my car breaking down or not starting up in front of my house. Eventually, our friendly conversations over the phone led to my finally inviting him inside my house. I would never forget that evening. My children were in Brooklyn with my family. I put on my favorite little green dress, trying to be cute, and thought a nice little dinner would be impressive. I thought I was ready to date again! Although I was saved, I was not fully completely convicted of the ways of the Lord. We were kissing, but then I got very emotional. I was crying and kept saying, "No, I'm saved. I can't go any further. I can't do this."

I was conflicted because there was a battle between my flesh and my spirit, but my spirit was strong, so I said to him clearly, "No, I can't do this!" Moreover, I wanted him to console me more than anything else. In retrospect, I was in no shape to date because I was not healed from my bitter divorce. Everything went another way. The kissing led to him taking what he wanted right there in my living room. I had a camera set above the armoire and even forgot that my camera was there!

I had no intention of telling anyone, much less using the camera footage to prosecute. I was vulnerable, embarrassed, and ashamed. What makes it worst (my craziness), he came back again the next week and the following, but it was consensual. I didn't stop him or say no. Satan really had me for a minute! Then after the third time, this jerk had the nerve to tell me, "I'm unhappily married and live over there with my wife, but we are not really together. I just live there for now!" I was like, "Get the hell out of my house and lose my number quick!"

I got tested, thinking that I had contracted something from him, but God protected me from that. I am so grateful. The nonconsensual sex wasn't even the bigger issue. It's what happened four years later in 2020, in the middle of grieving the death of my dad that shook me, broke me to the core, and ultimately strengthened my faith like never before. My poor choice during that three weeks encounter with that man caused life-changing consequences. But God was in it all along because he allowed it to happen. He was teaching me a great lesson. If that man did not disclose that he was married, I would have probably continued a bit more with fornication, which many believers overlook as if it's an acceptable sin.

I learned, lesson number one, don't be so quick to open your heart for it might give the devil easy access to slip right in. The Bible tells us in Proverbs 4:23, "Keep thy heart with all diligence; for out of it are the issues of life." I was not firmly rooted in the Word as of yet, not knowing the power of that particular Word. I slowly learned to test people's spirit and wait to see where they are coming from. It is not what people say, but rather, what they do that matters.

God knows where I am weak in the flesh and where the enemy could and would infiltrate my mind, body, and soul. He tells us in His Holy Word, "Do you not know that your bodies are temples of the Holy Spirit, who is in you, whom you have received from God? You are not your own; you were bought at a price. Therefore honor God with your bodies" (1 Cor. 6:19–20 NIV). I needed to go through that hard trial from which God brought me out to be wiser and stronger, so I could become the uncompromising disciple He has called me to be.

Why bother to talk about the rape? Who on earth would believe me? I thought, especially since I continued on with him after it happened. But years later, I realized it is not a matter of whether one believes me or not. It is a matter of getting free from the hurt, guilt, and shame of what happened, which was not my fault. After hearing the testimony from the F.A.C.T.S podcast, I was so empowered that I knew this was the season to release what has been hidden and share my story. Talking about rape could be a very blurry topic, especially if it did not involve violence like gunpoint restraint or other drastic measures. Indeed, I should have been dressed more appropriately and covered up to avoid sending out a seductive message; however, it was not my fault nor ever the person who is sexually violated against their will's fault. No means no, and I said no.

CHAPTER 8

2020: From Darkness to Light

BACK IN 2017 I was at a pizza shop near my house and ran into the man, the one that sexually violated me. I had already forgiven him. I learned a very vital lesson about what God was delivering me from and understood that he was a broken soul. Hurt people hurt people. Apparently, he moved out of that house, and I never saw him again. However, the aftermath or consequences of my encounter with him in 2016 changed my life in 2020 and forever!

In the spring of 2020, his wife's brother or nephew (I'm not quite sure about the people in that house and the nature of their relationship) came out of jail. All I know is that I looked out my window, saw the young man on the porch smoking, and said to myself, "Oh no! Trouble is back. This is the last thing this block needs right now!" When we first moved to Cambria Heights, we were so impressed with the quietness. The only time there was any form of noise was when he, Trouble, was around. Everyone on the block knew that he was the culprit for any disturbances on our quiet street. Oftentimes, the police would come around looking for him. Not too long since we moved there, we stopped seeing him, and the noise dissipated. When months led to years and we didn't see or heard him from the block anymore, we knew the police found whom they were always looking for. In his absence, the block was quiet and peaceful again until the spring of 2020. I'm not sure, but I have a feeling he was one of the prisoners that got early release from jail due to the rapid spread of COVID-19.

January 2020 was a hopeful month. Many people were still hopeful and made their reservations about the double blessings and double victories to come. What we didn't see coming that first week of January was the pandemic that would shake the world and affect every living soul on planet Earth.

It was like living in a horror movie, watching people by the hundreds die suddenly each and every day. The nightmare continued when I would drive by a local hospital and see the large refrigerated trucks parked outside of the hospital, serving as a makeshift morgue. We were devastated and grieved to hear about our very young friends who lost their father on Friday and then their mother four days later early on in the pandemic. We pitied and sympathized with them, not knowing we were going to be mourning too one month later.

We didn't see it coming. It happened so suddenly. One day, Dad started throwing up blood. We got him to the same local hospital down the block where bodies were housed in the outside refrigerated trucks. He was diagnosed with the coronavirus, but after two weeks in the hospital, he got a bit better and was sent home. The next day, he started breathing funny; it was difficult, and he couldn't eat anything. He had no appetite, lost about 25 pounds in a week, and refused to even drink water. After a week home, his breathing got more difficult, so the ambulance took him right back to the hospital.

My brother Andrew, whom I believed God ordained to be a nurse and serve at a time like this, was the strength for all of us! Nurses and essential workers, in general (that's anyone who risks their lives to serve others), are often overworked, underpaid, and certainly not celebrated as much as they deserve!

Andrew, the youngest sibling, would leave his overnight shift at his hospital in Manhattan, exhausted and overwhelmed, then show up, every day at the hospital in Brooklyn where my dad was hospitalized. At first, he showed up to check on Dad and make sure he was well taken care of. Because he had on his uniform and nurse's ID, the hospital made an exception for him when no visitors were allowed. Andrew ended up cleaning Dad himself because the nurses were so overwhelmed by the substantial number of patients assigned to each of them. They were not able to handle minor care, such as washing up or changing adult diapers on patients consistently. Every day, after leaving his shift, Andrew would make his way to the hospital and stay for almost another shift. He was no longer there just to look after Dad. He saw the need because of the lack of enough nurses and volunteered to help them out. Under no circumstances would any hospital allow an outside nurse to come in and help out, but New York City was the epicenter of the pandemic, and hospitals were strained beyond measure, so another unofficial exception was made.

To put aside your own needs and put your emotion in check to serve and help others to live while clinging onto hope for yourself to live is what many doctors, nurses, nursing assistants, EMTs, paramedics, and essential workers did during one of the darkest times our generation has witnessed. In my opinion, that is one of the greatest examples of humanity, showing forth your light in the midst of darkness! I salute my brother Andrew for his bravery and thank God for giving him the grace, strength, and courage to help his patients and for taking great care of Dad!

> **In all the work we do, God commands us to let our light shine before men, that they may see our good works, and glorify our Father which is in heaven.**
> **—Matthew 5:16 KJV**

My brother would visit Dad every day and update us on his prognosis. He was improving, talking, and getting better, but Andrew kept telling us, "Be prepared. Be prepared because although he looks better, things could go another way!" At that time, there was no vaccine to control the spread and so my dad was given hydroxychloroquine, which is really medication used to treat malaria. Dad had an adverse reaction, which shut down his organs; and in less than two weeks, in May 2020, my dad passed away. Funeral homes were overbooked, and so we waited over a month to bury my dad on June 8, 2020.

It was in this time period, after my dad's sudden passing that I experienced the trial and test of my life. It was one of the darkest periods of my life, but then, there was light! I went through some of the stages of the grieving process and came to full acceptance quickly. Perhaps it is because Dad got saved fifteen years ago, after a massive truck accident and minor stroke, and felt at peace, knowing He was in God's hand.

Dad always prophesied that he was going to live up to the age of seventy-five. We would correct him and tell him to stop saying that, but every year after his birthday, he would confess that he is going to live up to seventy-five years old. When Dad passed, he was seventy-five years old and seven months! The Bible tells us in Proverbs 18:21, "Life and death are in the power of the tongue." Perhaps Dad knew something we did not know, and God obeyed the words of his confession. Nevertheless, words have power!

Sticks and stones can break our bones, but words *can* certainly hurt us! We must be careful and intentional about what words we use when speaking about our lives and others.

I felt at peace because, during Dad's last days, he was at peace. He wanted to go. In fact, he was released from the hospital for the first time, because he progressed very well. He was never on a ventilator. We prayed and wanted him to live and believed in God for his healing. But Dad had no will to continue; he wanted to go.

It's easy to blame his sudden death on the unknown effects of the medication, but the truth of the matter is, Dad prophesied the number of years of his life on Earth. He suffered a lot in the last four years of his life and wanted to go on. Although we mourned and accepted his transition with grace, it is imperative that everyone understands that words have power, and we must use them to speak life over our circumstances.

Just a few weeks after Dad's passing and before his burial, my niece Jafira was staying with me. One Saturday morning, I heard a loud crash, the sound of a car hit by another car. I immediately said to myself, "I hope that wasn't Jafira's car. It sounded like her car got hit!"

I looked out the window to see the driver reverse his truck a little, then accelerated the gas to hit the back of her car again, knocking off the bumper. Then he did the same and knocked off her left side view mirror and sped off. I saw a glance of his face from the side and knew right there and then it was no accident! I have seen him before. He was one of the visitors who visited Trouble, the neighbor fresh out of jail!

My niece and I got dressed and race outside to pick up the rear bumper and other pieces that were lying in the street. When we got outside, I heard the neighbors from that house all cheering about the hit. It sounded like they were celebrating a touchdown at a Super Bowl game. That was how loud they were that early Saturday morning. I didn't explain this to my niece because it didn't even make any sense. I knew instinctively, intuitively that her car was hit, and it was not an accident. I remember them watching from their step the day my niece moved her car from down the block to park closer to my driveway. Her car was parked across the street from my driveway for three weeks. I had no idea though that the demon from down the block and across the street, the one I referred to as Trouble, would have ordered a hit on my niece's car. Trouble was back, and this was just the beginning!

A few weeks later, on June 29th, the day after my daughter's birthday, I allowed her to go out to dinner with her best friend. This was the very first time my daughter was going out since the lockdown in March 2020. I dropped her off at her friend's house and made my way to Brooklyn. My mother and son were in the car. Terrence was in the backseat with his seatbelt on, and my mother was in the passenger seat. After exiting the Belt Parkway, I began to slow down before coming to a full stop at the red light. Out of nowhere, a car slammed into the back of my car, causing me to slam into an SUV that was in front of me. My entire front hood and bumper got damaged and as also the back of the SUV that I slammed into. After the hard hit, the driver sped to the left-turn lane to get out from behind me and sped two blocks down away from my view. I was able to see that the car that hit me was an old gold Toyota with New Jersey paper tag plates with the number 722. I was not able to get the remaining numbers on the plate. Thank God, my daughter was not in the car because, if she were, she would have been in the backseat without her seatbelt on as usual and would have gotten seriously hurt. God knew I would have had this encounter, and I believe her outing was divine protection.

I decided to call my friend Karen, whose husband's best friend is a detective and always helpful. I also called 911, wanting to get the police to come to file a report. I waited for a long time. About fifteen minutes after the hit, I notice on the other side of Pennsylvania Avenue in the direction going back to Queens, the same gold Toyota with the same markings on the side slowly driving by. The driver was on the phone! I jumped out of the car quickly in hopes of getting the rest of the plate numbers, but it was too late. We waited for over an hour for the police to come. The detective friend called a precinct on my behalf to inquire why we were waiting so long. Apparently, another crime within that jurisdiction required more police attention. But the police finally arrived and were very gracious to me and the driver of the car who I slammed into.

It was there and then that I knew my life and my children's lives were in jeopardy. Again, I knew the hit was intentional. I didn't have the evidence yet but knew it was from the neighbor down the block and across the street. I began to explain everything to the detective friend in hopes of his intervention. He is known to be very helpful to even his friends' friends. Unfortunately, for some strange reason, he didn't want to get involved. He was getting ready to retire and said the courts are not even addressing minor crimes due to the strain on cases from the pandemic.

The hit on my car occurred a few weeks after my spiritual assignments increased, and I was blessed to begin serving as a ministry leader positioned as Minister Theresa. I have heard many times that the greater the anointing, the greater the attacks, but this was something that truly tested my faith on a whole different level. When the detective friend could have easily made a few calls and inquired about Trouble's probation officer which he must have had coming out of jail, but did not want to get involved and, when the camera footage from the gas station nearby didn't cover that part of the street to show the car with its plates, I knew I was in a serious battle, spiritual warfare!

My car was damaged and was in the car repair shop for three and a half weeks, costing over $7,000 worth of damages. Thank God, I had full coverage! My niece's car on the other hand was not fully covered and cost me over $2,500 in repairs. Thank God, none of us were hurt! I was driving a rental car for almost a month.

One Saturday morning I was loading the rental car with bags. It took awhile to load my car. I noticed that across the street a white car was double parked in front of the neighbor's house, and the driver was the same dude that hit my car, which is why I was using a rental. I quickly came out of my driveway to take a look at the full plate numbers. Sure enough, the car sped off and again I only saw 722, the first three numbers on the New Jersey plates. It was the same driver, the same New Jersey paper tag plates, but a different vehicle. The devil was getting ready to follow me again, and this time hit the rental car that I was using. I went right back into my house and did not leave for many days!

I called up my friend, Theresa B., and she prayed with me about my situation. I also called up my other friend, Millie, who invited her friend, Pastor Carol, to intercede as well. Sometimes we can't always burden our leaders with every problem we face because they already have their own warfare to deal with and, at the same time, must cover all their members at all times. The moment we make up our minds to surrender to God and have His will in our lives, inevitably, a life of spiritual warfare takes place! Because of this, it is imperative that we have a few intercessors in our lives who are able and willing to pray for us at the drop of a dime. We too must be available to stand in the gap and intercede for others as well!

I was in a state of total fear. I could not have prayed myself out on my own. I'm so grateful for the friends I have and whom I can call on in the middle of the night to intercede.

I was so fearful that my sisters, Maria and Andrea, who live nearby, became very concerned and visited to bring food and check on me. I did not know how to explain to them that the attack on my life was the result of an involvement I had with my deceptive neighbor four years ago. Nevertheless, I thank God for revealing the enemy and protecting me from another hit-and-run accident.

Another time, I was watering the lawn in front of the house. Trouble comes out, stands in the middle of the street, and begins to talk on his cell phone loud enough for me to hear, "Yeah, the b——tch is out! I wanna get in the basement, but she got somebody down there."

I kept on watering the lawn and pretended as if I didn't hear him. From that moment on, every time I watered the lawn, which was every morning, I would have my cell phone in my pocket, prepared to record his conversation. Soon, I realized he was just a coward, trying to inflict fear to get me to move!

As a minister, we are called to serve, encourage, and lead others to Jesus Christ. We are called to live a life that glorifies God and to put our faith in Him. I knew, without a shadow of a doubt, that I was called to serve, but at that time, I was living in fear.

I spent most of the summer driving and, at the same time, always looking back or through my rearview mirror to see if someone was following me. I was beyond fearful. I was traumatized. My daughter would say, "Mommy, stopped looking backward while you're driving!"

I would pull over and allow "suspected" cars to pass by because I was filled with fear and wondered if the car behind me was going to be another hit.

At the same time, I was given my first preaching assignment in the sermonic series entitled, "Keep the Faith." God gave me the message, which was taken from Romans 8:38 and 39 KJV, "For I am persuaded, that neither death, nor life, nor angels, nor principalities, nor powers, nor things present, nor things to come, nor height, nor depth, nor any other creature, shall be able to separate us from the love of God, which is in Christ Jesus our Lord."

I was used on that Sunday to encourage others to keep the faith no matter what we go through, especially when the enemy tries to destroy us in hopes of separating us from God. Right after that, the Lord began to talk to me the way your best friend does. He told me, "You just preached about keeping the faith, and now it is time for you to live it!" I knew I had to release fear and allow God to work faith in me! I knew I had to do something.

The next day, I started a three-day fast. Through His word, I started to encourage myself. Every time I got into my car, I began speaking God's word. I prayed, "For God hath not given us the spirit of fear; but of power, and of love, and of a sound mind" (2 Tim. 1:7 KJV) when I woke up, when I got into my car, and before I go to bed. That word gave me the push to shift from a fearful being to a more faithful worshipper. My walk by faith has never been the same.

Soon, I learned to pray strategic prayers. One night, I was on YouTube, searching for protection prayers to hear and meditate on during the night because I had difficulty sleeping. I stumbled upon Apostle John Eckhardt's *Prayer That Rout Demons* book, which was in an audio version. I played that prayer every night for at least two weeks straight. I began praying that the work of the enemy against my life and family be canceled in the name of Jesus. I began praying for God to deliver me from every scheme, plot, and plan the enemy cast against me and my family and send it back to the pit of hell where it came from in the name of Jesus! I prayed Ephesians 6:10 over my life every day and night. I commanded, in the name of Jesus, that every fiery dart the wicked one launched against me and my family be sent back to where it came from! I became what they call a prayer warrior. God's word empowered me and answered prayers prevailed. Fear was lifted. Hallelujah!

After a few weeks, as I continued to play the audio prayer overnight, I started to hear very loud screams coming from down the block across the street, the neighbor's house. Every night, I noticed bright lights from every window of the house all night and loud screams of "No no no! Ah, ah!" continued as if someone, a grown man, was getting a serious whipping. This went on for weeks. I recognized, through a revelation, what was happening. The man's voice was Trouble. He was frightened at nighttime. For some reason, he needed to keep the lights on. Could it be that the fiery darts that he cast against me reverted to him?

Early one Saturday morning, I heard him screaming again, "She gotta go! That b--tch got to move!" Only this time, I was not afraid! I was concerned about his state of mind! I was no longer afraid and got very concerned about the screams and bright lights that were always on all night. I started to pray! I felt sorry for him and the entire family. I asked God to have mercy on him and his family. I would see the look on the older woman who lived there in the morning, looking very distressed, most likely from not sleeping because of the lights and screams. God revealed it and reminded me in His word, "Do not gloat when your enemy falls; when they stumble, do not let your heart rejoice, or the Lord will see and disapprove and turn his wrath away from them" (Prov 24:17-18 NIV).

Another Saturday morning, Labor Day weekend, I was loading my car in preparation for the long day's journey. I was getting ready to attend our church's second annual Praise in the Park/executive assistant pastor's birthday celebration at the same local state park where I joined the church one year before. I knew it was going to be a long day of driving. First, I had to leave Queens and stop in Brooklyn to get some food and borrow a shopping cart to load juices. Then I was going to make my way to Staten Island to pick up Kimone and my niece. Then I had to drive back through Brooklyn and Queens (BQE) to Manhattan to get to the Bronx where the Praise in the Park was taking place. Then after the celebration, I would have to do the same thing, leave the Bronx, drive through Manhattan, then Queens and Brooklyn to get Kimone home in Staten Island, only to drive back through Brooklyn to get back home in Queens.

As I was loading the car, I started to pray for traveling mercy and for God to give me the strength to endure the day. I was loading and praying verbally. I unintentionally began praying in the spirit, not realizing the neighbors were passing by. When I finished, I saw them looking down at the ground. I saw fear in their eyes. My prayer was for traveling mercy, but for some reason, God intended for them to hear it. Not too long after that encounter, I was coming out of my house and saw Trouble on his porch. He quickly looked down and then went back inside. I saw the fear he had, and I didn't feel good about it.

Some people cling to wealth and positions, which enable easier opportunities for getting things. However, that's not true power because that kind of power is only dependent on your current status. Having people afraid of you is also false power, vainglory as well!

The ability to love people who hate you and pray for people who use you is a sign of having true power.

It takes the Holy Ghost's power to sincerely love your enemy! Jesus models that for us when he prayed for and forgave those who accused him and ultimately died on the cross in Calvary for us and all of humanity. I now understood what God was doing when I fasted, and he led me to the Word, "For God has not given us a spirit of fear, but of power, and of love, and of a sound mind."

He gave me the power to love, and with that, I was able to pray for Trouble, who I now refer to as the brother that was broken, in hopes that he already received his deliverance.

He was broken just like the boy that tried to penetrate me when I was seven years old. He was broken just like the super who molested me when I was ten years old. He was broken just like his brother-in-law, who sexually assaulted me and misled me about his marital status. He was broken just like me and many of us who are believers and still in need of deliverance.

Many of us are broken and don't even realize it. Many of us walk around depressed, distressed, hurt, and wounded. I know these feelings very well. I also know that Jesus is our healer and deliverer. If we yield our wounds to him, He will heal us according to His will. Perhaps you are burdened and broken right now. May I encourage you to say this simple prayer with an open heart:

> Father God, I come to you in the name of Jesus
> Just as I am broken, hurt, and in need of healing
> Your Holy Word says, "Many are the affliction of the Righteous, but the Lord delivers him out of them all"
> Oh God, I ask you right now to heal me from the past and present hurt
> that has left me
> wounded in my soul
> Oh God, I ask you right now to deliver me
> from emotions caused by trauma
> and emotions that linger in my spirit and cause toxicity to myself and others
> Oh God, I thank you in advance for

healing and delivering me from
The power of darkness
and showing me
your marvelous light
In Jesus's mighty name, I pray. Amen!

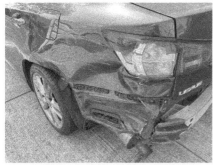 

My niece's car that got hit by the neighbor in May 2020.

Nurse Andrew during pandemic   My ordination to Elder
                                   with Overseer Collins

My mom, third from right, with seven out of ten siblings, June 2020.

Jamaica, 1978. Ma, Ingrid, me, and Denise.

My daughter and son, 2022.

Ma and Dad on my wedding day, July 2008.

CHAPTER 9

Just Being

AFTER THAT TRIAL, which was really a spiritual battle for my spiritual growth, I received confirmation about selling the house and moving out of Queens. I used to travel to Maryland over the weekends to visit my sister. Oftentimes, I would go away for the weekend only to return home and find mayhem in my backyard. During the months leading up to the season when my neighbors were provoking me, I came home and found a dead bird under the table in the backyard. One time, I returned home from spending the weekend with my mother and found three huge animal bones strategically placed in a straight line and all in my driveway, and the glass top table in my backyard was completely shattered.

It crossed my mind many times to sell the house and move, but the thought of uprooting my children's lives made me reconsider. The neighbors no longer provoked me, and I was complacent about where I lived. But with me, when God needs me to move in the direction in which He wants me to go and I continue to be reluctant and operate in stubbornness and self-will, He shakes things up.

It was around February 2021 when my other neighbor, who normally would have helped me shovel snow, passed away the summer before, so I had no one to help me shovel. I was not feeling well one day but had to get outside to shovel and then sprinkle salt on the sidewalk to prevent pedestrians from slipping. It was then that I made up my mind for sure and said, "This is my absolute last time shoveling snow! I can't do this anymore. I'm selling this house!"

Sometimes in life, we just have to make up our minds to agree with God about what He is trying to do in our lives so that everything else will flow in our favor according to His will!

After I made up my mind to sell, one week later, over the winter break when I was in Maryland visiting my sister. I received a call from my other sister Kimone. She tells me one of her best friends wants to buy a house in Cambria Heights and that she told her to call me because it's such a big coincidence that she's looking and I'm selling!

I had no recollection of my sister bringing her friend to the house a few times before. Upon getting the phone call, she explained to me that she already knows the house and has a strong interest in purchasing it. She also informed me that her paperwork was in order, already having her preapproval for a mortgage, and she was ready to go! By March 2021, bank paperwork was submitted, and by June 2021, the house was sold.

Obedience is better than sacrifice. When we obey God, He blesses us in such a way that others around us reap from the blessing as well. The selling of the house and my sister's friend's purchasing of the house was such an easy and effortless transaction. We did not need a broker or real estate agent, nor did I have it on the market for anyone to view. One of my concerns was having strangers view the home while still residing in it. Thank God that did not happen. It was a simple private purchase, a wonderful blessing for both parties.

Moving back to my mother's house has been a blessing for the family as well. God never blesses us just for ourselves. My mother and I both needed each other's help. Since my dad's passing, her house has had an empty feel to it. I also struggled with finding some alone time because my children are always, and I mean always, with me. Living upstairs from my mom gives me time to go out without worrying about finding a babysitter. Also, she has someone in the house to drive her around if needed. Another blessing from selling the house and moving out of Queens is that I was able to purchase another as an investment property in Maryland, my favorite, easy-to-get-to getaway! God was just waiting for me to be obedient to His will and move forward!

And Samuel said, hath the Lord as great delight in burnt offerings and sacrifices, as in obeying the voice of the Lord? Behold, to obey is better than sacrifice, and to hearken than the fat of rams.
—1 Samuel 15:22 KJV

After all that I experienced in the nine years that I have been saved and walking with God, all I want to do is be who God has called me to be and please Him. I understand that He not only called me, but I am a chosen vessel. Many are called but few are chosen. We are chosen when we say yes and live a life completely obedient to His will. He called me with the gift of discernment accompanied by the power to intercede in the spirit. That's why my early stages of serving were frustrating. At that time, I doubted what I discerned and didn't know how to intercede.

Being a vessel of God is not easy because it comes with a life of spiritual warfare. But we overcome by the blood of the lamb and the Word of our testimony. As vessels, we must know that the weapons will form but shall not prosper. With Jesus, we have the grace to endure because the Bible tells us that after you have suffered a little while, the God of all grace, who has called to his eternal glory in Christ, will himself restore, confirm, strengthen, and establish you. We ought to expect trials, challenges, pain, setbacks, disappointments, and heartache, but we are anointed to handle them. While going through the storm of life, it doesn't always look or feel good. But because God knows everything about us and is in control of everything we could ever face, in some way, somehow He works everything out for our good.

I thank God every time my haters show up, and believe me, they show up and show out! I no longer worry about the haters. They are there to remind me that I am still blessed and favored! Instead of battling with them, it is just better to pray that they will experience the blessings of God to love and not hate.

Sometimes our blessings show up as a burden. The Bible tells us in Luke 12:48 NIV, "From everyone who has been given much, much will be demanded." Sometimes these burdens are difficult and painful, but at the end of the day, it is a privilege to be alive and an honor to be used as a vessel for God to carry out whatever He purposes for His glory.

It is God's grace and only His sufficient grace that I continue on just being, just walking with the call of God on my life. I continue on in God because I don't have a choice. I continue on in God because He won't let go of me. I continue on because I have witnessed over and over again in the midst of our darkest situations, even when it feels like God is not with us, He shows up. God shows up because He loves us and He is patient. This means there is always hope. If we just wait a little while, eventually, we will see that out of darkness, God's magnificent light prevails.

I desire to be a great mother, an effective educator, a loving family and friend, a faithful servant of the Lord, and a wife again if that is God's will, but I cannot accomplish anything without help from God. And I don't want anything that He has not ordained for me. I need him every day, every hour, every minute, and every second. Without him, I am helpless and can do nothing!

Poems of Praise

I Give It

Oh, Father God,
You are my everything
I am so grateful
And appreciative
For what you did and
What you are still doing
Words can't even begin
To express this magnificent
Thing
Your wonderful spirit
That you placed within
Me
It is a hidden treasure
That cannot be measured

This Holy Spirit
That you blessed me with
Comes with a supernatural gift
It has been revealed
That I can use these hands
To help and heal
I will pray in the spirit
As I serve and worship
Under this God-given headship
Because you transformed my life
Indeed a different creature anew
My purpose here on Earth
Is to love and serve you

From this day forward
I declare and make this pledge
To give you my weaknesses
Which in turn are your strength
I give you my heart, my soul,
And mind
'Cause your grace and love
Cannot be denied

For when I refused you
And abused your holy name
Still, you were merciful
To answer when I called
On Jesus's name
You saved my son in the physical
Ordained that circumstance
To save me in the spiritual

You blessed me
Exceedingly, abundantly all that I could ask
Or think of in this life

Have your way with me Lord
As I present myself as a living sacrifice
'Cause faithful is your love, oh God,
And nothing can compare
That you are God and God alone
Your goodness, I will declare
Thank you, God,
I give my all to you
Use me to fulfill
Your will
And the glory goes to you

I Am

I am a sister who was
Yanked outta darkness and
Shown the light
It is a privilege to fellowship
With God
Through Jesus Christ

It is a gift to stand before you
As a sister in Christ
And share my testimony
That touches on my new
Spiritual life

I am a work in progress
Guided by the Holy Spirit
This path was chosen for me
God's plans and purposes need
Not be defended
As long as what I do
Is transcended
To others in which
I love and serve

It's about giving and loving
And caring and serving
It's about something that is much
Bigger than myself
Or any personal yearning

I am a sister who will love
I am a sister who will bless
Yes, I will love you
Even if you want to hate on me

I will bless you
Even if you judge me
I will love you even when
You accuse me
I will bless you
Even though you try
To use me
I will lift you up
Even when you try to knock me down

I will love you with all sincerity
Because God's Word gives me clarity
He says, "Love your neighbor as you love yourself"
That is God's commandment
I will stand before him free and confident
During Judgment
Day

But, in the meantime,
I pray and I pray and I pray
That you bless me when
I walk into the things
That the Divine
Says are mine
With my full name on them

See, I am here for a sacred and
Spiritual reason
Better yet, we are all here for a sacred and
Spiritual reason
It starts with this season
Of walking into God's holiness
Of walking into God's righteousness
Of walking into God's blessedness and faithfulness
Of walking into a life that expresses

True love and unity
And rebuke whatever the so-called enemy
Might think or say about me

See, I am like a tree that's
Planted by the river of waters
So any weapon, plan, or plot
That anyone tries to form
Will not befall me
Because I am covered
You are covered
We are covered
By the Blood of Jesus

We are covered by the blood of Jesus
And that gives us peace and
Protection
And strength
To even love our enemies

Yes, I can, yes, I can, oh
Yes, I can
Why
Because I know who I am
Who I am and whose I am

I am a child of God
Blessed with the Holy Spirit
Blessed with the blessings of Abraham
Galatians 3:14 says through Christ Jesus
We are blessed with the blessings of Abraham

So I know I am
Blessed abundantly

Blessed with His Grace
And all sufficiency
I am blessed because
I am a sister in Christ

Something to Say

It is your third pastoral anniversary
And I have something to say
This poem is a God-given inspiration
Delivered to you on this
Special day

We give thanks to God for
Sending you
A faithful spiritual teacher
We give thanks to God for
Choosing you
A committed righteous leader
We give thanks to God for
Blessing you
With life just one more day
We give thanks to God for
Using you
To bring forth His Word
Every week on Sunday

It is your third pastoral anniversary
And I have something to say
You made a declaration on
The first Sunday
Of the 2015 New Year
But then something happened
To shake your faith and
Instill Fear
And probably made you question
Whether it was God's voice
That you really hear

THERESA TULLOCH

But the goodness of the Lord
Will always prevail
With Jesus as your advocate
You certainly have the victory
That is why you overcame
That adversity
And are here with us
Celebrating this third anniversary

It is your third pastoral anniversary
And I have something else to say
You deserve all the things your
Heart desires
Despite what some people don't know
But feel the need to say

Continue to serve the Lord
And keep doing all the things you do
'Cause he's made a clear path for you
With new blessings awaiting you

It is your third pastoral anniversary
And I have one last thing to say
To God be the Glory that
You are celebrating with us
On this special day

I Repent

It took a long time
To write this poem
Didn't know where
To begin
Thought I'd be inspired
To write about restoration
But came up blank
Whenever I picked up
The pen

Until God said
Make that declaration
After all, this is about
Your salvation
God said I am waiting
For your confession
You must first repent
Before I restore anything

He said
Repent so I can start
A brand-new thing
I want to release you
From that bondage
You know, that thought
That has you obsessing
And stressing
In the midst of your confusion
Is a hidden blessing
Eyes have not seen
Ears have not heard
What I have for you
Is spiritually discerned

First, you must repent
In addition, be content
With what I have started
Acknowledge that you were
Wrong
And I, God,
Will mend what you have
Broken

Therefore, I stand before you all
To make this true confession
It was the malice of my heart
That got the best of my emotion
Leading to a moment
Of what we call a fall
From His glory and grace
But His spirit that lives within me
Gives me the courage
To get up from off my face

Thank you, heavenly Father
For giving me, Jesus
It pleases me
That you are transforming this
Sinful heart
You perfect all that concerns me
By granting me a fresh, new start
To become the woman you
Ordained me be

Holding on to your Word
And promises
Knowing that you have
A greater plan
Yielding to your directions

Even when I don't fully understand
Learning to trust you, Lord
And refrain from using my hands

God said, repent and wait
Child, you have just started your
Walk of faith
Obedience is better than
Sacrifice
Bearing this heavy burden
Will lead to your eternal life

For the suffering and pain
Don't compare to when you
Enter through the narrow gate
Pray and keep your heart
Pure from sin
Ask and it shall be given
That I protect and hedge you in
Remember, Jesus died on
Calvary's cross
So when you repent
You are forgiven
He said I must love
My brothers and sisters
Despite what they say
Or think
This journey is not about my
Opinion
But rather about
Representing Jesus for the souls
I am supposed to win
I Repent!

So Suddenly

It happened so suddenly
A blessing from God
Dropped right out of Heaven
It is a force compelling me
To take hold of this great
Blessing, a once in a lifetime
Gift to behold
A manifestation of a lifelong
Dream, desire, oh yeah
My secret goal
Right in front of me
It happened so suddenly
This attraction that
Is completely magnetic
It is so powerful
That each day, it is
Overwhelming me
Bringing joy that is
Incomparable to what
The world has never given me
You see
It happened so suddenly
What was a jovial joke
In response
I suddenly looked up
With a sheepish smile
And there you were
Looking right back
Into my eyes
Oh Lord
My knees got so weak
I didn't know whether
To laugh out loud

Or fall on my face and cry
Then, suddenly, I left your
Presence in a drunken state
Wondering if you're gonna
Talk to me and spark our
Very first date
Yeah, suddenly, I realized
This encounter is more
Than just a casual thing
Let's keep the faith
Enjoy each other's company
In excitement to what
Our connection might bring
To others just like us
Believing that all
Things are possible
In God we trust
Suddenly
The most precious gift
Of all will show up
when you least expect it
Praise God, I promise to
Love, cherish, and protect it
Suddenly, I'm feeling
Something that people
Say is just plain and simple
Love
Wow, what a blessing
Thanking my faithful father from
Above
Suddenly

Sisters in Christ

Sisters in Christ
I'm calling you out
Where are my sisters
Who love from their hearts
And bless with their mouths
They praise the Lord by
Making loud shouts

I'm talking about sisters
Like Bella, who dances in the aisle
Take one look at her, she makes
You smile
And my sister Debra, who stands up and
Says Amen
In the silent sanctuary
Just before the sermon begins

Blessings to all my sisters
Who are saved and try to live right
Let the love for one another
Shine with the spirit of Christ
'Cause in this church, there is
No place for hate
With that type of sentiment
One will never make it through
The narrow gate
To the kingdom of heaven
And so, I'm telling
You
There is no reason
For envy
Or rivalry
Or trivial competition

Or false accusations about
A so-called opposition
Don't you know that
When you judge me,
God will judge you
Don't you know that
You can't stop
What God has started
Don't you know that
You can't block
What God has anointed
Don't you know how the story
Ended
When Joseph's brothers
Pretended
That he was dead 'cause
They envied
His gift of interpreting dreams
Don't you know how the story
Ended
With Jacob getting the blessing
That Esau thought should have been his
Don't you know how the story
Ended
They conspired against him
But God was on his side
So Daniel walked out of the lion's den and
Worshipped the Lord

No one can take what God has
For you
So give a sister your blessing as
She does what God calls her to do

No one can touch
What the divine says are mine
No matter how hard anyone tries
God has spoken
His Word is unchanging
His promises will not be broken
So I hold up my Bible
As a token
Of defense
When I'm faced against
The Goliath around me

The Holy Spirit will always overpower
The spirit of evil
That is tricky and deceitful
Know that God will use
Whom He chooses
To call back His people

So we got to be ready
And love one another
As we love ourselves
Because that is God's commandment
We can't afford to fall short
On the Day of Judgment

Sisters in Christ
I'm calling you out
For the rest of this journey
Let's make coming to church
Be about love
For God and others
So our Father from above
Can see
That we are joined together

In love and unity
We show love by supporting
Each other's ministry
We must love
So our Father from above
Can see that we strive
To lead a holy life
That honors God's commands
That were brought to us through
The one and only Savior
Whose name is Jesus Christ

How Do I Say Goodbye

How do I say goodbye?
I am not going to even try
Because, deep down inside,
I know this can't be
The final end
According to God's precious
Word, we shall see
You again

Only wish I had
Not taken time for granted
And spent time with you
More often
I'm not going to
Say goodbye
Although as these words
Are expressed
I can't help
But pour out tears
Of sadness
And cry and cry
And cry

Thank you, Lord
For the privilege of
Having dad in our lives
He's in your hands
Right now
So I pray that
One day, we will see him
On the other side
Where lies your promise
Of Eternal life

ACKNOWLEDGMENTS

I GIVE THANKS TO you God for this work and for allowing me to share my story. This is all for your praise, glory, and honor! Thank you, Father God, for the trials, tribulations, and victories that are intertwined with this journey of life and my walk of faith with you. This body of work is truly a testament to your grace, mercy, and faithfulness.

All my life, I preferred writing over speaking because public speaking has always made me feel uncomfortable. It is a great privilege and honor to share my story in writing with you. Thank you for taking the time to read this book. I pray that you have been encouraged and blessed.

I want to give a big and special thanks to my wonderful family. Our family is too large to thank everyone individually. I thank you, Ma, for always allowing me to be myself and loving me. I thank you, Tracy and Terrence, my beautiful children, for inspiring me. You both are my undeserving gift from God! I thank you, dear siblings: Dwight, Wayne, Andrea, Ingrid, Robert, Tristan, Denise, Maria, Kimone, and Andrew. You are all unique, loving, and supportive always. Please share your stories too! I thank you, Auntie Pansy, a.k.a. Ms. Senior, and Aunt Ivy for your encouragement in the Lord and for leading me to salvation. Thank you Jafira, my niece, a.k.a. Godchild, for being there with me during my darkest days; and all my nieces, nephews, cousins, aunts, and uncles here and in Jamaica for your understanding and support.

I am so grateful to have the greatest friends in the world. You all keep me grounded, laughing when I should be crying, and level-headed when sometimes I feel like I'm going to lose it. I feel blessed that each of you is connected to my journey whether you are mentioned in this book or not. Thank you, Monica, Pamela, Nicolene, Millie, Rhonda, Theresa B., Jackie, Christine, Karen, Gloria, Shawn D., and Sharon L. for all your love, prayers, and support during the good and difficult times.

Thank you to my pastor, Bishop Alicia Collins. It is your obedience to your calling that allowed me to understand my divine purpose. I thank God for your life. Thanks to my Empowered People in Christ NY family. It is an honor to serve the Lord alongside each of you.

Thank you to my work family from NYC Health and Hospitals Corporation, Hunter College, P.S. 59, P.S./I.S, 178, and my new family at ENYFA.

CPSIA information can be obtained
at www.ICGtesting.com
Printed in the USA
BVHW052153291222
655298BV00013B/111